CONSCIOUS CONSERVATION

LESS DOING, MORE BEING

DR. HAYLEY R ADAMS

DR. HAYLEY ADAMS
the compassionate conservationist

THANK YOU FOR YOUR SUPPORT

A portion of the proceeds from each book sold will be donated to support the Silent Heroes Foundation. www.thesilentheroes.org

For more information about Dr. Adams please visit www.drhayleyadams.com

Listen to her podcast, Conservation Without Borders

Follow her on social media @drhayleyadams

I dedicate this book to those courageous souls who devote their lives to passionately protecting, defending, and preserving wildlife; to those who feel their soul ignite when immersed in nature; to those who had a seed planted in their hearts as children, beckoning them to nurture their love for the wild; and to those who have indelible memories etched into their minds of time spent in the wilderness. This is for the conservationist in each of us.

May we all rediscover the love that connects us to that special place in nature for which there is no substitute. May we all nurture the self within that knows, inherently and completely, the value of connecting with nature and all her beings.

This book is for anyone who dreams of a brighter future for planet Earth. Those who work diligently and tirelessly to improve themselves and the world around them. Those who demonstrate compassion for all species and suffer as they witness the continued loss of our wild spaces and wild beings. You are all Silent Heroes to me. May you become your own Silent Hero in this journey.

I would like to give special thanks to my editor, Erica Ellis, for the necessary scrutiny of my words that helped to transform my manuscript into a book, and to Hillhouse Graphic Design for turning my vision into reality with a gorgeous book cover. Thank you to everyone who has played a pivotal role in my life; the tragedies and triumphs have led me to exactly where I needed to be.

Finally, I dedicate this book to Dr. Jane Goodall, whose compassionate heart and inspirational life have always served as my beacon of hope.

PREFACE

I am by nature an introvert. As a young child, I was painfully shy and most comfortable spending time quietly by myself. I was often immersed in my own mind, a cavernous place for me to explore. From a young age, I knew I was destined to work with animals. Whereas I wasn't always at ease around people, I was completely at home in the presence of animals. I adored spending time in nature. Naturally, I gravitated toward a career in healing animals and became a veterinarian. Over the years, I have had the privilege of pursuing my passion relentlessly, helping animals, researching wildlife disease, conserving wildlife and wild spaces, and supporting people in becoming good stewards of wildlife. These days my time is increasingly devoted to the preservation of all that has been naturally created in this world. Ironically, this requires me to spend the majority of my time in front of a computer rather than outside in nature. I have spent the past two decades researching, teaching, fundraising, advocating, and working diligently to preserve what is fast slipping through our fingers like sand through an hourglass.

I still have a long journey ahead, yet I have come far from the frustrated conservationist I once was. I didn't know how to navigate the seemingly never-ending struggle to find solutions to the overwhelming challenges of modern conservation. I resented humans for their destructive influence on Mother Nature. I often felt like a contradiction in myself, proclaiming the value of what one person could do to change the world, yet feeling as if I was powerless against so much negativity. But this was only due to my limited viewpoint. I could only see life through the filter of my past, my experience, and my own narration. I hadn't yet discovered the limitless supply of awareness, intuition, and compassion that would transform me from an unconscious conservationist to a conscious one. I hadn't yet discovered my inner self.

We are human "beings," not human "doings." Our journey on earth is an opportunity to connect with our true essence and to connect deeply and purely with other beings. This connection is neither forged nor strengthened by how much we do; rather it is strengthened through our growing awareness of who we truly are and of our connection with the universe. This is the key to the future of conservation— a conscious, intuitive, and compassionate approach to restoring balance to our planet.

PART I

INTRODUCTION

Wilderness is not a luxury but a necessity of the human spirit. ~Edward Abbey

This book was created to be the antithesis of what has become commonplace in modern conservation. It serves as an antidote to the doom and gloom surrounding our global environmental crisis. If you are disillusioned, frustrated, angry, grieving, feeling helpless or hopeless, feeling compassion fatigue or burnout, feeling overwhelmed and unsure how to meaningfully contribute given the magnitude of the challenges we face in modern conservation, read on.

This book will help you transform your perception of and your approach to conservation through focusing on the inner transformation necessary to practice conscious conservation. It is not a summary of the various ways in which we humans are destroying our planet and its beings, and thus ourselves. It is not a criticism of the discipline of conservation as a whole. Rather, it is a call to turn away from the onslaught of negative rhetoric, beliefs, and practices that no longer serve us in conservation. This book is not an attempt to uncover the many conservation techniques in practice today, other than using a few as illustrations. For as much biodiversity exists on the planet, there is as much diversity in conservation.

Conscious conservation is radical in its reliance upon the power of the human spirit to restore global ecological balance. It is an individual approach with collective benefits. Its power comes from within and therefore does not rely on the extraneous forces that we ultimately do not and cannot control. What we can do, however, is inspire transformation within others, as our own transformation causes a ripple effect in those around us. Over time we will begin to see the change around us that we have experienced within. By transforming ourselves through conscious conservation, we will create the world we wish to see through the power of inspiration rather than through force.

Once the tenets of conscious conservation are learned and applied, there will be no desire to waste precious energy blaming and shaming those we perceive as the enemies of conservation, and no need to engage in defeatist tactics that spread fear, anxiety, frustration, and anger. We will be filled with inspiration, creativity, and compassion, and we will lead and inspire others with this energy.

Conscious conservation requires a mindset shift into "willingness." At this level, our minds, hearts, and souls begin to open to possibility, and we are no longer dictated by doubt and fear. We no longer expect to see the worst in our world, but begin to have the willingness to be open to the other side of the story. It is here that miracles occur.

When we allow ourselves to see things with the clarity of the present, rather than the filter of our own past perception, what once was seen as an obstacle now becomes a challenge. And all challenges are opportunities for learning the lessons, for growth, and for transformation.

Conscious conservation is revolutionary in that it utilizes a new framework for the human species. This framework removes the label of victims and villains, the mentality that blames ecological destruction on a certain group of people such as poachers, corrupt politicians, or money-hungry businessmen. When we utilize this victim mentality, we blame the problems we see on the actions of others and thus it becomes us against them. We villainize others, make ourselves the victims (or the heroes), remain blameless, and thus are in no position to take positive action or to find an innovative solution. We must be willing to drop this mentality and to reframe the problems we see in conservation as challenges that have no winners or losers.

This in no way implies that we agree with the actions of those who are harming our planet, her wild spaces, and wildlife. We will still hold accountable those who commit egregious acts against conservation. However, we will no longer do so with contempt in our hearts or with a blame-and-shame approach that leaves a toxic divide between us and them. We will uphold the tenets of conscious conservation that enable us to protect and defend nature with compassion, intuition, acceptance, and awareness. We will no longer engage in the zero-sum battle. This shift in perception requires willingness, but once it occurs, we begin to view the human species as a part of the very ecosystems we wish to protect rather than as separate from them. Once we do this, the context of conservation itself changes and endless possibilities emerge.

Conscious conservation can be utilized as a complement to any facet of conservation, including policy development, raising awareness, endangered species preservation, human-wildlife conflict, deforestation, combatting wildlife crime, or climate change. It is a skill set available to all conservationists regardless of education or experience. Although the book has a slant toward wildlife conservation, the tenets of conscious conservation are universal and flexible and can be adapted to work with any challenges faced by modern conservationists, whether they be on land, in the sky, or in the sea.

One of the most beautiful and critical aspects of adopting this skill set is the inner transformation that occurs. It allows us to reconnect with our love of the wilderness, rekindle our passion for conservation, and let go of the tragic stories of the past that we hold on to. We will stop distracting ourselves with the noise of the latest eye-catching conservation headlines that broadcast the worst possible news. We will be able to focus on what is relevant, important, and pertinent, and act with clarity and certainty to effect positive change. We will no longer be in a state of frustration, anger, or hopelessness, as we will now have a means to process the realities of the day in a healthy manner, leading to productive discussion and action, rather than to "engage and enrage" (i.e., to become engaged in negative dialogue or thought processes with colleagues or through social media, and to become enraged with those whose actions harm Mother Nature).

We will stop seeing the world as tragic. We will no longer see humans as the enemy. We will no longer blame others and feel helpless to contribute or force people to comply through restricting their actions, fearing that it is only a matter of time before compliance is breached. We will recognize the power within to become the change we wish to see in the world.

My hope is that this book will serve as a catalyst for significant global change. It was written to encourage us all to first look deep within, before looking without, to the root cause of the challenges we face as conservationists. I hope to inspire each of you to recognize that, despite the crises, we are never without hope. That in order to heal our planet, we must first heal ourselves. Then we must be willing and courageous enough to allow the inner miracles to come forth.

This book represents the evolution of conservation to a new paradigm, one that combines mind and mindset to produce what I have coined "conscious conservation." This book serves as an instructional guide that will transform you, and thus the world around you, through the tenets of conscious conservation.

UNCONSCIOUS VERSUS CONSCIOUS CONSERVATION

We must be the change we wish to see in the world.
~Gandhi

Unconscious Conservation

Our inescapable reality: daily we hear of global destruction, loss of habitat, and climate change. We are living amidst what has been termed the "sixth extinction."[1] We are losing countless species from the planet each day, many that we have yet to identify and describe, much less introduce to the world at large. How can we be expected to save what we haven't yet discovered? We are faced with the increasing pressures of habitat loss, climate change, disease outbreaks, threats to endangered species, loss of biodiversity and ecological health, and human-wildlife conflict, all at the hands of the most ecologically destructive species on the planet: humans. We know all too well the anthropogenic (human-caused) stresses imposed on the world today. Both news and social media ensure we do not soon forget. We are bombarded with negative stories, harsh imagery, and doom-and-gloom messaging that serves to reinforce our collective feelings of anger, frustration, and helplessness. An overarching theme in conservation is the global lack of sustainability of current human lifestyles. If we don't reverse the trends, the losses will continue, and the world as we know it will reach a point of no return. Are we destined to fail as the guardians of the planet?

Unquestionably, one of modern conservation's most pressing issues is that of poaching and the illegal wildlife trade. It is arguably the most maddening, disheartening, and troubling challenge we face in conservation today. As a result, conservationists have joined the ranks of soldiers in what is commonly referred to as a "war on poaching"; a war for which we are underprepared, underfunded, and underequipped.

In addition to the war on poaching, there is a growing divide between conservationists and anyone who knowingly or unknowingly participates in global ecological destruction, including politicians, big business, corrupt government officials, those who drive the illegal wildlife trade, and anyone else who desecrates our wildlife and wild spaces. As conservationists focus on saving the planet, we cling to our "rightness," unable to see a clear way forward where both sides benefit. This results in deep animosities, deep wounds, and two sides: us versus them, right versus wrong, winners versus losers. We have come to view conservation as a zero-sum game. In order for conservation to win, someone or something must lose.

What You Focus on Expands

Conservationists are invested in the preservation and conservation of nature's wild spaces and wild beings. To affiliate oneself as a conservationist is to identify with the desire to live in harmony with the natural world. This is a desire for peaceful coexistence with the wilderness and its beings. Conservationists are advocates for nature. Yet our roles as conservationists have become increasingly more hostile and our position as defenders of the wilderness ever more tenuous. Negative rhetoric has become all too common in modern conservation. We talk about the war on poaching; the fight against climate change; the loss of habitat, species, or biodiversity. This terminology can be found at the forefront of many conservation campaigns today and is prominent in our social media feeds. We are bombarded with negative messages over positive ones. Do you feel the weight and power of these words? Warring, fighting, and losing. What happens to us psychologically when we are exposed to such rhetoric in our daily news feeds and in conversation? What is all of this emphasis on negative terminology doing to us individually and collectively, not to mention to conservation itself?

Over time we become hardened and bitter, and we perceive reality through the filter of negativity. We become fatigued by the constant reminders of loss. We develop compassion fatigue and cannot bear another tragic tale. We are increasingly angered, frustrated, and exhausted by the fight to protect and defend nature. We develop bitterness and hatred toward nature's "foes". We blame them and shame them for the problems we face. We dig our heels in deeper and resolve to fight harder. Yet the devastation continues.

We have become unconscious conservationists. We are focused on fixing, fighting, reacting, restricting, and controlling. This is energetically draining and it is not a sustainable approach to problem-solving. Our foes are resistant to our fighting, to our reactionary approach, to our need for control, and to the restrictions we attempt to push upon them.

We have practiced unconscious conservation far too long.

Unconscious conservation is an unsustainable way of creating lasting positive change for the planet. As unconscious conservationists, we rely on a zero-sum mentality of right and wrong, winner versus loser, and an us-versus-them mentality. We focus on and share negative news, which promotes a fear-based approach to conservation. We are reactionary, with a tendency toward anxiety and depression from a focus on the tragedies of the past or the disasters of the future. We attempt to control or force our foes to comply with regulations and restrictions based on a "can't do" mindset, and we blame, shame, and label others as "part of the problem." We identify and focus on obstacles and problems, and attempt to fix only the more superficial issues or surface problems. We desire violent or forceful approaches to protecting wildlife and wild spaces. We have a mentality of lack and compete with colleagues for funds, recognition, and even for claiming a species as ours alone to protect and save. We rely exclusively on logic, reason, and facts in the decision-making process and ignore intuition and social, emotional, cultural, psychological, and economic aspects of conservation challenges.

The Conscious Approach to Conservation: Definition and Tenets

Definition: conscious conservation is an evolution of conservation that combines the modern holistic approach with awareness, intuition, and compassion for the global challenges we face. It is a transformative way of "being," rather than "doing," conservation, whereby the individual embodies that which they envision for the world. It places humans within the global ecosystem rather than outside of it, and thus emphasizes a focus on humans as a species to bring back into balance in order to restore the balance of the global ecosystem as a whole.

Conscious conservation requires three significant shifts: a shift in your point of view, a shift in your mindset, and a shift in your approach.

A shift in point of view by:

- Viewing all humans as potential conservationists
- Including humans as an interdependent component of the ecosystem
- Seeing opportunities and challenges rather than obstacles

A shift in mindset by:

- Cultivating a mentality of abundance
- Focusing less on the ego and more on the inner connection to all life
- Protecting Mother Nature and viewing conservation challenges from a place of compassion rather than anger

A shift in approach toward:

Humans:

- Focusing on solving human-based problems as a necessary focus of modern conservation

- Empowering humans within the challenge to become part of the solution
- Promoting the community-based approach to conservation that involves options for "can do" rather than "can't do," as well as the sustainable utilization of natural resources, including plants and animals
- Preserving biodiversity, restoring healthy ecosystems, and promoting the value of free-ranging wildlife as beneficial to human livelihoods

Raising awareness and education:

- Seeking to inspire rather than use fear- based doom and gloom

Addressing conservation challenges:

- Asking why and taking a deep dive into the root causes of conservation challenges
- Balancing science with intuition to solve conservation challenges (science + intuition= conservation in action)

As you learn about the shifts and the tenets of conscious conservation, I encourage you to focus on identifying the areas in your own work where you are stuck in an unconscious viewpoint, thought pattern, or approach to conservation, and work to shift into a conscious viewpoint, thought pattern, or approach. In time I believe you will see a significant change in yourself as well as in your life, your work, and your impact on conservation.

Summary

Takeaways

- We have become unconscious conservationists, focused on fixing, fighting, reacting, restricting, and controlling
- We have come to view conservation as a zero-sum game with winners and losers
- As unconscious conservationists we see only the problems, we blame and shame others, and we attempt to control them in order to achieve compliance
- Unconscious conservation is an unsustainable way of creating lasting positive change

Questions for reflection

1. Do you identify with some of the characteristics of an unconscious conservationist?
2. Are there aspects of modern conservation that have you feeling frustrated, angry, helpless, or hopeless?

Less doing, more being

Becoming a conscious conservationist is a journey that shifts us from the unconscious "doing" approach to the conscious "being" approach to conservation. We begin to abandon "doing" conservation by fixing, controlling, reacting, and forcing and over time can transform into "being" conservation through accepting, creating, inspiring, and empowering.

Begin to recognize the ways in which you are operating unconsciously as a conservationist, doing things without thoughtful intention or purposeful action, ignoring your gut instincts, or taking action from a place of anger and bitterness (which in reality is more of a reaction than an action).

Become cognizant of the ways in which you are reacting to what is happening in conservation, whether what you see on social or news media, or the actions of your colleagues. Begin to notice whether your motivator for conservation is primarily internal or external—are you driven by internal forces such as your passion or your desire to create positive change, or are you driven by external forces such as a desire to stop the destruction and to stop those who are harming Mother Nature? Simply becoming aware of these characteristics is a powerful first step in transforming them.

PART II
A SHIFT IN POINT OF VIEW

Our perception is our reality. The filter with which we perceive the world has a significant impact on our thoughts as well as our actions. If we have suppressed sadness, we often see the world as a sad place and tend to focus on the sad circumstances of the world. If we have suppressed anger, we see the world as an angry place.

When we view the world through the filter of negativity, we see obstacles, we see the ugliness in the world, and we focus on the destruction. We blame people and circumstances for our anger and frustration. This holds true in conservation as well. We see conservation as a zero-sum game with winners and losers. We view humans as the problem. We focus on the problems in conservation. We place a magnifying glass on these things, as we are programmed to seek out what we believe to be true in the world around us. Although there is also plenty of positivity surrounding us, we are unable to see it.

When we focus on blaming others for the problems we see, we give our power to change the circumstance away to those we blame. We minimize our ability to contribute and make an impact while maximizing their ability to contribute in a detrimental way. So long as we view the world through this perspective, we will not see positive change. In order to see positive change, we must first be willing to shift our point of view. Conscious conservation begins here.

There are three areas of conscious conservation where a shift in our viewpoint is necessary in order to begin to transform ourselves and the world around us. The first is a shift in the way we define a conservationist, followed by a shift in the way we view humans in general, and finally, a shift in the way we view the state of conservation today.

SHIFTING OUR PERSPECTIVE OF A CONSERVATIONIST

hat you do makes a difference, and you have to decide what kind of difference you want to make. ~Jane Goodall

Historically, the term conservationist was reserved for those independent, adventurous souls willing to live under challenging conditions in the relative solitude of the world's wild spaces, gathering data, recording information, and reporting findings back to the civilized world. By and large, the world they explored was a mysterious and abundant place filled with an endless supply of species and biodiversity.

Today's conservationist cannot be so narrowly defined. We wear a variety of hats and have adapted to fit a variety of niches. Conservation today represents a myriad of scientific fields, incorporates a multidisciplinary approach to problem-solving, and consists of anything from field work to desk work. Today many conservationists, including myself, spend the majority of our time miles away from the wilderness we research, advocate for, and protect. Many of us are confined to our institutional headquarters in the developed world or spend months campaigning, fundraising, grant writing, and speaking to audiences in an effort to raise awareness and support. All of this takes us away from the wild spaces and species we work hard to protect.

Whereas historically conservation was reserved for those who made it a lifestyle, a sacrifice, or a career, today conservation has become a practice of the people, by the people, for the people. It can and should be a participatory discipline with roles for everyone to play, including advocacy, research and technology development, education, conservation medicine and the preservation of species, resource allocation and conflict resolution, and policy development and implementation.

A conservationist is therefore anyone who advocates for or acts on behalf of the protection and preservation of wildlife and natural habitats or who contributes to ecological health, biodiversity, preservation, or the restoration of nature through our choices and behaviors.

Any one of us can play a significant role in conservation, whether by working directly for organizations or institutions involved in conservation or by supporting conservation efforts through the giving of our time, tithe, or talents. The era of social media has truly revolutionized conservation such that everyone has a voice. Each of us has the potential to effect positive change as a conservationist, irrespective of our educational background, career or life choices, or geographical location.

In fact, some of the most memorable and innovative breakthroughs in conservation came from individuals who, at the time, were not yet considered to be conservationists. Dr. Jane Goodall was chosen by Dr. Louis Leakey to study chimpanzees despite the fact that she did not have a formal scientific education. She was chosen based on her observational skills, her conviction of character, and her intelligence. She has credited her ability to distinguish the personalities of the chimpanzees she studied, and thus to bring to light the emotional lives of wild chimpanzees, to her lack of formal scientific training.[2] This enabled her to use a more compassionate, intuitive approach to her research, and as a result, she changed the world of wildlife conservation. She has since become one of the greatest conservation leaders of our time.

Richard Turere is credited with saving lions from human-wildlife conflict by inventing a deterrent system of LED bulb fencing called "lion lights" that stopped lions from attacking his family's livestock at night. Richard was just eleven years old when he discovered that lions were afraid of moving lights shined toward them and developed this innovative solution to a growing problem of human- lion conflict in Kenya. His economical solution is also culturally appropriate, as the technology is readily available to livestock farmers throughout east Africa, where lion attacks on livestock are not uncommon and retaliation to lions includes poisoning and spearing them to death. His creative invention came about despite a lack of formal education in electronics or engineering.[3]

These are just two examples of "ordinary heroes"— individuals who utilized their intuition, combined with a love of nature, to transform conservation through innovation and an ability to think outside of the proverbial box. No time in history has provided us with more opportunity to make a positive impact for conservation. Conservation should be of the people, by the people, and for the people.

Summary

Takeaways

- A conservationist is anyone who advocates for or acts on behalf of the protection and preservation of wildlife and natural habitats or contributes to ecological health, biodiversity, preservation, or restoration of nature through their choices and behaviors
- Conservation should be of the people, by the people, and for the people

Questions for reflection

1. What challenges do you face as a modern conservationist?
2. What sort of conservationist are you? What are you "doing" in order to effect positive change? (We will work on shifting from "doing" to "being" as we go through the tenets in the book.)
3. What is your definition of a conservationist?

Less doing, more being

Shift your point of view and broaden the definition of what it means to be a conservationist. See donors or those who support your conservation efforts from the sidelines as partners. Perhaps at times you have felt as if you alone are responsible for enacting the change necessary to see positive results. Lessen the burden of your individual journey by viewing your colleagues, peers, friends, and family as a support system and a network for achieving success in conservation.

See the potential in everyone to make a positive contribution to conservation, including those people you may feel are largely contributing in a negative way.

Think about the challenges you face in conservation, and the role that humans play in contributing to those challenges. Begin to reframe those humans as potential conservationists, rather than as villains. What can be done to transform the way they contribute to conservation from a net negative to a neutral or net positive impact? Inspire others to take ownership of this identity as a conservationist and their ability to make an impact.

SHIFTING OUR PERSPECTIVE OF HUMANS

ou must not lose faith in humanity. Humanity is like an ocean; if a few drops of the ocean are dirty, the ocean does not become dirty.

~Mahatma Gandhi

It isn't difficult to understand that our hominid ancestors were an integral part of the ecosystems in which they lived. They foraged and hunted off the land for survival and utilized natural resources to construct shelter and make fire. They lived interdependently with the natural world. They were a distinct part of the ecosystem and their actions had a direct impact on it.

Yet in modern times we view humans as largely separate from and removed from the natural world. We have constructed a false sense of separation through mass urbanization and heavy dependency on technology, agriculture, health care, manufacturing, industrial production, and systems engineering in order to survive. In truth, however, we are still dependent on the natural world for our resources and ecosystem services, or the ways in which humans benefit from ecosystems, such as food, water, pollination, and recreation. Our health and well-being is also highly dependent upon the health of the natural world. Our actions still have both direct and indirect impacts on global ecological health. Yet we have largely relegated ourselves to an artificial world where nature is simply a place we go to escape our urban lifestyles. Nature is something we enjoy for a short time while on vacation until we get back to our "regular" lives.

This distance from our primal connection with nature has implications far beyond the aesthetic. Our connection to nature is also a connection to our deepest selves, to our true selves. In nature, we are called home again. Nature allows us to relax, to rejuvenate, and to let down our walls and pretenses. In nature, there are no judgments or pressures. We are free to delight in "being", rather than "doing". Nature is essential for human health and well-being. Yet along the way we have disconnected from nature. We have become suffocated in the details of all that is wrong in the world. We have become burdened with the task of fixing. We are lost in our depression over the tragedies of the past and our anxiety over what may happen in the future. We have stopped seeing the beauty and only recognize the brokenness. This is a catastrophic flaw in our current strategy. How do we restore our collective connection with nature and thus rebalance the global ecology before it is too late? The answer lies within, so within we must be willing to go.

By living this way we are not only fooling ourselves, we are doing a massive disservice to conservation itself. We have made conservation an afterthought, something to support in order to satisfy the pleasure of "spending time in nature," or something to ensure that we can travel to exotic places from time to time to view wildlife. Over time, conservation became exclusive to a subset of the population that enjoys nature for her aesthetic value. Conservation evolved into a specialized discipline with a false pretense that allows us to opt out if we so choose.

The truth is, no one is immune from humankind's dependency on nature. All of humanity has direct and indirect impacts on the natural world. So why then is it acceptable to behave as if we have a choice? Why do we think we have the luxury of treating it as a pastime?

Because we have removed ourselves as humans from the ecological equation! Slowly, over the generations, agriculture allowed us to become more stationary and less reliant on hunting, gathering, and pastoral lifestyles. We began creating urban areas that allowed us to develop commerce and trading. We were pulled away from our primal connection to the natural world. We lost respect for our interdependent relationship. We took for granted the benefits of a healthy ecosystem. We began to use and abuse nature and to see ourselves as separate from her. This separation allowed us to deny to a certain extent that we are still interconnected and interdependent.

It may seem like a monumental task to reverse the trends and the damage currently taking place on the global stage. In reality, it needn't be this way. What is required is a shift in perception. A shift in understanding. A shift in our reality. A shift in our knowing and in our being. We must acknowledge our place as human animals, as a part of nature itself. We are part of the ecosystems in which we live. This shift is a powerful first step toward creating the world we wish to see, and it begins not by fixing the ecosystems we are separate from but by becoming a part of the ecosystems we must relearn to value, negotiate with, and respect.

By considering human beings as a keystone species in the environment, we begin to see ourselves in the same manner that we see wildlife species in terms of things like population health and management, conflict management, and behavior. We see ourselves as drivers of ecological change.

We live in an era of a global ecosystem where actions taking place halfway across the globe make an impact on local ecosystems. Our sphere of influence extends far beyond that of our ancestors. In modern conservation, our interdependency can be seen as having a global reach. Our greatest impact may take place in our backyards, our communities, and nearby parks and preserves, but our influence, and nature's influence on us, doesn't end there. It extends far beyond where we live and what we see. Depending on how often you travel, or the products you buy, the food you eat, and the sort of work or activities you participate in, your interdependency and thus your impact may reach much further.

Conservation generally places all fauna and flora except for human beings under the umbrella of protection. This is a dysfunctional framework. In reality, we are an essential part of nature. We are one with nature, whether we choose to acknowledge this or not. It is the law of nature itself. We are the species with the largest ecological footprint globally and the driving force behind all major modern global environmental and conservation challenges. Humans are severely out of balance ecologically. We must focus on restoring the balance of human populations, behaviors, and habits, in order to restore global ecological health.

Summary

Takeaways

- We have a tendency to view humankind as separate from nature
- We have made conservation an afterthought
- We must acknowledge our place in nature, as part of the global ecosystem

Questions for reflection

1. What are some of the negative ecological impacts of humans?
2. How do you view humans in the context of your work as a conservationist? Are they a nuisance or a problem? How can you begin to view them as part of a potential solution?
3. How can we begin to reintegrate humans into the conservation mindset?

Less doing, more being

Stop focusing on fixing a natural world that excludes human beings. When we fix the problems within our own species, nature will fix herself. Begin to place your focus on integrating humans into the global ecosystem.

Operate within a new paradigm where human beings are included in the conservation mindset. Accept reality as it is, rather than how you wish it to be. Denial or a mere desire for things to be different isn't enough to bring about positive change. Accept that humans are overpopulated and responsible for much of the environmental degradation we see today. You must also accept that all humans have fundamental needs that must be met, including food, water, and shelter, and that their survival dictates that they do what is necessary to secure these resources, which may include means that are detrimental to conservation.

Acceptance of reality does not equate agreement, nor resignation to current circumstances. It does however create space for opportunity to transform the situation. When you take action from a place of acceptance, you are more likely to include humans and their needs in your conservation planning. A conservation mindset that is inclusive of the human species is a game changer.

SHIFTING OUR PERSPECTIVE OF CONSERVATION

*E*very challenge, every adversity, contains within it the seeds of opportunity and growth.

~Roy Bennett

We are all born with a full complement of emotions that guide us through our life. These emotions serve a myriad of purposes such as bonding with others through love, keeping us safe through fear, and calling us into action through motivation. Emotion is a necessary, irrefutable part of being, and yet so many of us are largely unaware of our own emotional intellect. Emotional intelligence is the ability to identify and manage our emotions as well as to identify the emotions of others, and includes the ability to harness and apply them during problem-solving. When we fail to identify, process, and release our emotions in a healthy manner, we carry them with us through life without properly tending to them.

Emotion trapped in the body through suppression and repression is a catalyst for disease. The body doesn't distinguish between perceived and true stress, thus the stress we are exposed to, through negative media for example, has a cumulative impact on us.

We become masters at internalizing our emotions as well as our stress. We often don't even recognize we are stressed or living a stressful lifestyle. We become addicted to the stress itself, as well as to the negative media cycle.

We become accustomed to seeing graphic images of poached wildlife, and although we are horrified, we come to expect it. We slowly become immune to the images of violence in the media. Thereafter, when triggered with disturbing images or circumstances, we often desire to seek vigilante justice in an equally violent and gruesome way.

So what does emotional intelligence have to do with conservation? There is a high degree of frustration these days in conservation. We are by and large participating in conservation with a low level of emotional intelligence. We blame a variety of conservation foes such as corrupt officials, politicians, poachers, hunters, and "uncaring citizens." We become frustrated and angered by their actions. We hold on to our frustrations and pain over the ecological destruction we witness, and as a result we suffer. We recycle and ruminate over the pains of the past, and this prevents us from creating innovative, sustainable solutions moving forward.

In unconscious conservation, we are emotionally unintelligent and are easily emotionally triggered into a reactive state. It is from this place of reactivity and emotional chaos that we take action. Our world view is distorted by our own emotional filter. What results is an inability to problem-solve with clarity and presence, or to take action from a place of awareness and acceptance of things as they are. We continue to be emotionally triggered and are unable to move forward out of the modern conservation challenges we face. Thus the challenges persist.

Combine this with the predisposition for humans to gravitate toward negative news, and the media's desire to sensationalize in order to sell, and what results is a preponderance of negativity.[4] Yet there lies a world of positivity, hope, joy, compassion, and inspiration to be uncovered in conservation.

By increasing our emotional intelligence, we will bring calm into situations where it is needed, rather than emotional chaos. We will have clarity to focus on the issues from the perspective of awareness, rather than from an emotionally immature and triggered perspective. When we shift our mindset and adopt a conscious approach to conservation, we drop the negative filter of past perception and begin to see and accept things as they truly are, without labels or negative attachments. This allows us to brainstorm and problem-solve for sustainable, beneficial solutions to conservation challenges, and to act, rather than to react based on our chaotic emotional state.

Opportunities, Not Obstacles

Being conscious doesn't mean that we never see or experience negativity. That would be a false reality as well. It means that we drop the labels we have used to identify and categorize things in the world as good or bad, positive or negative, right or wrong. We begin to see and experience things as they are, neither good nor bad. We drop our attachments to how we wish it could be. We sit in awareness of the present moment. It is here that we stop clinging to past stories that tell us we are doomed to fail, and we let go of the anxiety about the limited time we have to change the future. We tap into our creative energy, our true inner selves, in order to find answers. What we find are circumstances that involve opportunity, rather than obstacles. We discover that obstacles only exist in our mind. It is a choice we make to attach a negative label to a present circumstance. If we can free ourselves from this negative labeling, we will open ourselves to the possibility that the opportunity exists for the benefit of all involved, as it is a teaching moment for those willing and open to learn.

This new way of thinking doesn't necessarily occur overnight. It takes time to deprogram our thoughts from years of dichotomous patterns such as good versus bad. It takes time to stop viewing humans as the problem, as enemies or as foes. Although it may feel comforting or even right to place blame where we feel it is due, it can also become a crutch that blocks us from moving forward with creative, innovative solutions that work for both humans and animals. If we devise solutions that benefit wildlife without regard for human need, cultural appropriateness, and attention to available resources and the limits of technology, the solution will not be sustainable, no matter how wonderful it may seem on paper. Humans must be viewed as a species within the context of the ecosystem, with dynamic needs and behaviors that influence the outcome. Instead they are often labeled as the problem, and thus the solution becomes narrow minded— stopping the problem. This typically results in a "can't do" approach: restricting them, punishing and penalizing them, or blaming and shaming them. And clever, resourceful humans will find a way around most "can't do" tactics, especially when their life or livelihood depends on it.

Once the tenets of conscious conservation are practiced, a shift takes place and we transition from seeing obstacles in our work to seeing challenges and opportunities. Now humans are seen as part of the ecosystem. They are included in the transdisciplinary process, which combines knowledge from multiple disciplines as well as the engagement of communities at the interface of the challenge, both in defining the problem as well as in taking action to remedy it. The challenge itself may be multifactorial, including logistical, financial/economic, behavioral/psychological, and cultural components. Research and design to overcome the challenge takes place, as well as field trials and testing to ensure that the solution is feasible, scalable, and sustainable.

Once the challenge has been framed, the conscious conservationist works with key locals to brainstorm creative and innovative solutions that are beneficial for humans, animals, and the environment. Humans are no longer viewed as bad or part of the problem. They are viewed as part of the solution.

The conscious conservationist begins to see all challenges as opportunities. We find the hidden lessons in each of these opportunities. It is an opportunity for growth, for change, and for positive impact, both for the conservationist as well as the people and wildlife affected. The opportunity now becomes a source of motivation, providing room for creativity and inspiration to construct a better reality.

The following examples illustrate the difference between unconscious and conscious approaches to conservation challenges. They also serve to illustrate the importance of applying cultural context to conservation challenges.

From conflict to coexistence:

Obstacle: Farmers in Kenya retaliate and kill elephants when their crops are raided. As a result, elephants become more aggressive. The community resents elephants and are less likely to protect them. The unconscious conservationist cares more about the lives of elephants than the lives and livelihoods of farmers and continues to see farmers as the problem. They think and problem-solve from this world view, utilizing the "can't do" approach, telling farmers what they cannot do, that they cannot harm or kill elephants in an effort to protect their crops. The conservationist continues to focus on how to protect elephants and educate the locals about the value of elephants. Here conservation takes priority over the livelihoods of humans.

Challenge: The conscious conservationist recognizes that crops are the communities' livelihood, and that elephants can wipe out an entire family's crops in one night, which is devastating economically and nutritionally. They strive to find a way to allow farmers to maintain crops without the danger and threat of elephants, thus allowing elephants to graze and roam without harm. The conscious conservationist includes humans in the ecosystem and understands that their livelihood is of critical importance. Rather than problem-solving with farmers as the villains, they maintain awareness of each side as neither good nor bad and brainstorm with locals to find innovative solutions that work for both humans and elephants.

Opportunity: Knowing that elephants are fearful of the sound of disturbed bees, Dr. Lucy King develops a beehive fence that protects crops from elephants, thus allowing humans and elephants to more peacefully coexist. As a bonus, bees are environmentally friendly and produce honey, an additional agricultural commodity that communities can either consume as an additional source of nutrition or sell for supplemental income. Because this solution engages farmers and relies upon community participation, farmers are now part of the solution. They benefit from crop protection and the additional nutritional and economic benefit of beekeeping, and human-elephant conflict decreases, benefitting both elephant conservation and human lives.[5]

From poaching to farming

Obstacle: Poachers in Zambia track and kill animals illegally to sell or consume and cut down trees to make charcoal for fires. The unconscious conservationist argues that we are losing precious habitat as well as threatened and endangered wildlife species and defines poachers as the problem. They problem-solve from this viewpoint and find ways to discourage poaching using the "can't do" approach, so that conservation takes priority over cultural traditions, economic hardship, and the needs and desires of local communities. They place restrictions on the poaching of firewood and wildlife, and the community is resentful of this restriction, as it offers them no alternative source for fuel or protein-rich food. The risk of non-compliance is not high enough to abstain from poaching, and it continues despite efforts to curtail it with restriction and education.

Challenge: The conscious conservationist accepts the reality that local communities have hunted this way for generations, and that bushmeat is a cultural delicacy and an important source of protein and income. They strive to find a way to respect cultural tradition and preference while decreasing or stopping the illegal harvesting of trees and the poaching of wildlife. Poachers are not labeled as bad, and thus the conservationist can brainstorm creatively, free of negative labels that bias in favor of the "good" side.

Opportunity: After extensive discussions with community members, it is clear that the primary reason for poaching in the village is to supplement income and to provide protein that is hard to come by in such a remote location where grocery stores and electricity are nonexistent. Dr. Dale Lewis of Community Markets for Conservation (COMACO) devises a business model whereby poachers agree to turn in their weapons in exchange for shares in a community-based poultry and goat co-op. This serves the needs of the people quite well, and poaching drops significantly. Community members themselves become part of the solution. Additionally, the community benefits from a reliable, sustainable food supply, a boost to their local economy, and preservation of the local habitat and wildlife.[6]

From hunters to guardians

Obstacle: Historically, Maasai warriors of east Africa hunted lions in order to gain status and to protect livestock from potential predation. In the last few decades, as human populations have risen, human-lion conflict in east Africa has increased, primarily due to lion attacks on precious Maasai livestock. In retaliation for killing livestock, warriors will often hunt and spear lions, or community members will lace a livestock carcass with poison to kill lions, contributing to the decline in the region's lion population. The unconscious conservationist blames the Maasai for the declining lion population. They problem-solve from this viewpoint and find ways to discourage poaching using the "can't do" approach. They place restrictions on lion killing and expect compliance. There is no effort to provide an alternative solution, and livestock killing continues. As a result, the Maasai continue to kill lions, as the risk of non-compliance is not as high as the consequence of losing cattle.

Challenge: The conscious conservationist accepts the reality that local communities have hunted lions this way for generations, and that it is an important cultural tradition. The loss of livestock is also extremely damaging to the community, both economically and culturally, as livestock is highly revered by the Maasai. They strive to find a way to respect cultural tradition and preference while stopping the killing of lions.

Opportunity: Understanding the cultural significance of both lions and cattle to the Maasai, Stephanie Dolrenry and Leela Hazzah took the suggestion of local Maasai and transformed former lion hunters into lion guardians. The concept is simple yet innovative—to recruit former lion hunters, utilizing their knowledge and skill for tracking lions, to act as watchdogs, alerting herders to move livestock in response to a lion sighting. Thus they also act to directly protect lions. The charity Lion Guardians was born, and it has helped boost lion populations and enhance the livelihoods of the Maasai by protecting their valuable herds. Additionally, warriors learn to read and write so they can monitor lions and record data. They also act as community leaders and mediators, preventing retaliatory killings when livestock is attacked. They carry a strong sense of pride over their role as guardians of lions.[7]

Summary

Takeaways

- In unconscious conservation, we are emotionally unintelligent and are easily emotionally triggered into a reactive state
- The conscious approach to conservation requires calm and clarity in order to take positive action
- See obstacles as challenges, and they will become opportunities

Questions for reflection

1. What issues in conservation are emotionally triggering to you?
2. When we make humans the problem in conservation, what generally happens as a result?
3. What are the current problems in conservation that could be transformed into opportunities?

Less doing, more being

Now that you have identified a few problems in conservation, focus less on fixing the problem that you see and reframe it as a challenge to tackle. If you had previously identified humans as part of the problem, reframe the challenge without placing blame on anyone involved in the problem. Consider their unique perspective and needs as well as that of conservation. Why do they behave in a way that is detrimental to nature?

Look for the opportunity within the challenge, as this will bring about more opportunity for positive change. Focusing on the problems you see does nothing to transform them and only magnifies the problem. Devise a solution or solutions to the challenge that are beneficial for both humans and conservation. Now you are ready to take action and have become a part of the solution.

PART III
A SHIFT IN MINDSET

Now that we have begun to shift our point of view about conservationists, humans in general, and the state of conservation today, we have created a bit of mental space and energy to focus on the next necessary shift—the inner transformation that brings about a shift in mindset. The conscious approach to conservation requires us to transform our inner world in order to transform the world around us. This transformation won't happen overnight, but is a journey that will always have room for growth and improvement. It begins when we transform our mentality of lack and learn to see and experience abundance around us. Next we focus less on our ego and more on our deeper connection to the universe. We now begin to cultivate compassion toward all aspects of conservation, including its challenges and its foes. This compassion allows us to become positive advocates for conservation.

A MENTALITY OF ABUNDANCE

I don't fix problems. I fix my thinking. Then problems fix themselves.

~Louise L. Hay

What You Believe, You Perceive and Receive

The thoughts we think strongly influence our emotions, and thus our actions and their outcomes. What we believe to be true tends to manifest in the world around us. Thus what we believe, we perceive and receive. If we believe the world is a difficult place, we perceive it as such, and thus receive difficulties throughout our lives. Someone who believes the world to be full of lessons for growth and transformation receives these same circumstances as opportunities for growth rather than as difficulty.

This belief system holds true for unconscious beliefs as well as conscious ones. We hold our truths energetically such that our energy speaks louder than our words. Others can sense our energy, including animals, who are often more in tune with energies than humans are, such as the dog who bristles and barks when a "friendly" acquaintance enters the room. The dog is no fool. He is not discriminating against this person for no good reason. He is merely reading that person's energy and doesn't like what he senses. That person can have a smile on their face and attempt to talk sweetly to the dog, but this doesn't mask the negative energy surrounding them.

Our minds can deceive us, but our bodies and our energy reveals our truth. We all carry unconscious beliefs that have been instilled throughout our lives. Some of these are known as limiting beliefs, which hold us back from obtaining the success or happiness we seek. Common limiting beliefs are related to self-esteem or self-worth: I am not good enough or I don't deserve it. Many have a limiting belief that relates to lack in this world. We may believe, whether consciously or unconsciously, there exists a finite amount of something we desire, whether it be money, success, recognition, or even happiness. This limiting belief shapes our thoughts, our emotions, our behaviors and actions, and thus our outcomes. We operate from a place of lack rather than abundance. We believe that for us to have or to achieve, it must be taken from someone else, or that if someone else has or achieves, there is less to receive. It is similar to the zero-sum mentality we have discussed where in order for one to win, another must lose.

Lack or Abundance

When we operate from a place of lack, we create feelings of jealousy, we compare ourselves to others, and we compete for what we desire. This is a negative energetic state that leads us to behave as if our peers or colleagues are in competition with us, so that in order to have what we need or want, we must take from them. This is operating from a position of force.

In conservation many nonprofits operate from this place of lack, in competition with other charities for funding and support, comparing themselves to similar charities, and fearful for their own survival. This weakens their potential to bring about positive change in the world, as it not only wastes precious energy, but it limits their viewpoint so that they only seek that which others have already received. Thus there will never be enough to go around because of their belief in a limited supply.

The opposite of lack is abundance. Having an abundance mentality means we believe that an infinite amount of what we desire is available to us in the universe, whether it be funding, support, resources, solutions, or career success. When we believe that we have the power to create that which we desire, we experience feelings of generosity rather than jealousy, we have no need to compare ourselves to others, and we no longer need to be in competition with anyone for what we know we can manifest. The focus then shifts from an outer forced effort to an inner powerful intention in which we trust that, so long as we follow our own unique path, we will receive what is meant for us. This is operating from a position of power.

As conservationists, when we operate from a place of abundance, we feel kinship with our colleagues, rather than competition, and can celebrate the successes of others, as we know it contributes toward the greater good of conservation. We do not compare ourselves to other conservationists, instead focusing our energy inward, tapping into our unique skills, abilities, and creativity in order to become the best version of ourselves. We play to our strengths and work on our weaknesses. We manifest what we need through connecting with others who appreciate our worth. We know there is an abundance of support in the universe so long as we stay true to our passion and purpose. The abundance mentality can be cultivated by recognizing that there is infinite potential in the universe.

Summary

Takeaways

- What we believe, we perceive and receive
- Have a mentality of abundance and work in concert with peers, not in competition

Questions for reflection

1. Do you view conservation as a zero-sum game?
2. Are there ways (conscious or unconscious) in which you are in competition with your peers for resources, funds, support, or perhaps even recognition?
3. Are you operating from a place of lack or abundance?

Less doing, more being

Remove your focus from what others are doing in conservation and focus on your own unique skills, abilities, and passions. Become aware of any negative thoughts, doubts, or limiting beliefs in your mind regarding your work in conservation or the future of conservation.

Recognize that these thoughts are not truths, but if you entertain these thoughts, even in your subconscious mind, your mind and body believe them to be true. These hidden beliefs and doubts will hold you back regardless of how badly you wish to succeed. Write down these limiting thoughts as you become aware of them and, each time you become aware of their presence, replace them with an opposing thought of positivity or abundance. If your limiting belief is that we cannot save a species from extinction, you would replace it with the belief that there is always hope, that Mother Nature is quite resilient, and that humans have accomplished incredible feats in history, including saving a number of species from the brink of extinction. It takes effort at first but will soon become second nature, and your negative thoughts will begin to dissolve.

Take action from this place of abundant thinking. Become the person who sees abundant opportunity to achieve success in conservation. Remove your limiting beliefs, and you will remove the limitations that block your ability to problem-solve for solutions to the challenges we face in conservation.

LESS EGO, MORE ECO

ou have to leave the city of your comfort and go into the wilderness of your intuition. What you'll discover will be wonderful. What you'll discover is yourself.

~Alan Alda

The Thinking Species

Many of us spend the majority of our lives in our own heads. We narrate life as it happens to us, talking to ourselves without noticing that we never take a break from our thoughts. From the moment we wake until we fall asleep at night, our minds are talking, thinking, playing and replaying scenarios of the past, and imagining scenes of the future. Human beings evolved to rely heavily on our cognitive abilities. Thought itself is a prized attribute that has allowed us to develop complex communication and expression. We have, however, come to rely so exclusively on our cognitive ability that for most of us it completely rules our lives. We identify primarily with our mind and our thoughts, which dominates our sense of self. We underutilize our soul, our spirit, and our intuition, thus depriving ourselves and the universe of the tremendous power that lies in our inner beings. We recycle old conversations and scenes in our mind, running them over and over, or we project scenarios in the future that distract us from our present life. We go through life this way in a fog, largely unaware of what is going on around us.

Additionally, we are addicted to using technology and social media, which take us away from the present moment. These momentary distractions prevent us from tapping into the power of our own awareness.

The ego

The ego is a false self-construct that each of us develops as we go through life. The ego is built upon the beliefs we hold about our personality, our traits or talents, and our skills and abilities. We root ourselves strongly in this identity to uphold our self-confidence and help us relate to others in the world through comparisons of better or worse than or like and unlike. Thus we rank ourselves in an endless cycle of comparison and this feedback fuels our ego and self-image. You may identify yourself as easygoing or hardworking, as a member of a particular religion, as someone who enjoys a particular sport, or even as a conservationist, all based on what you do, your beliefs, and your likes and dislikes. All humans have an ego. It is an inherent by-product of our cognitive evolution. In order to tap into our true inner selves, we must develop an awareness of the ego itself and recognize that we are not merely our thoughts. We are the awareness behind the thoughts. The observer of the thoughts. The presence that exists in the space between thought.

When the ego is in charge, we ruminate endlessly on our thoughts. We tend to "think" our emotions rather than feel and release them. This means that we analyze, justify, and argue our position as it relates to feelings of anger, hurt, disappointment, judgment, and righteousness about a viewpoint. It is the little voice in our heads that is self-critical. Often we don't even realize it is there. To counteract that inner critic, our ego must overcompensate by finding worth externally and by acquiring status in the world through being better than, having more than, being the best-looking, the strongest, or the smartest, for example. This requires constant feedback from peers in order to reassure the ego that it is true. Thus the ego seeks endless validation from others. This need for external validation often results in fishing for compliments and reassurance and leads us to being easily hurt, offended, and angered.

What does this have to do with conservation? In conservation, many become engaged in the competition for resources, for funding, for the spotlight, for support, and for recognition. This is the playground of the ego. When ego dominates, the focus shifts from working toward the greater good—for biodiversity preservation and restoring ecological health—to winning, recognition, success, and even a desire to be seen as a "conservation hero."

The ego in conservation

Ego emerges in:

- Politics—through the exertion of status, ruling by force, the desire to gain and maintain power, or the desire for personal or economic gains over the greater good
- Corruption—through deceit, the desire to win or gain advantage through dishonest means
- Poaching and ecological destruction—through greed, the

desire for money or natural resources, or the divide we create between good and evil or right and wrong
- Conservationists—through the desire for recognition as a savior of wildlife or wild spaces, a desire for the spotlight, or in competition with our peers
- Nonprofits—through the desire to further a funded agenda rather than the greater good, or in competition with other nonprofits
- Research and academia—through the desire for acknowledgment of our wisdom and our discoveries, in competition with colleagues for funding or recognition as an authority for our area of expertise, or to be recognized for having more knowledge than others

We also see ego as attachment to iconic species that we identify with more so than others because we attribute certain anthropomorphic (human) characteristics to them such as beauty, strength, or personality. Think of pandas, lions, and elephants. They receive more attention, news coverage, funding, and thus protection than other less "lovable" species. This is an example of the human ego setting a conservation agenda based on what will get more exposure and funding by appealing to our inherent bias to save and support more aesthetically pleasing wildlife species. It is much harder to garner support for species that have been vilified by humans such as certain reptiles or bats. This leads to an imbalance of biodiversity and a loss of ecological resiliency. Each species has their place ecologically. We cannot judge other beings based on our humanness alone. They are sentient beings with inherent rights to exist simply because they exist. Nature doesn't make mistakes. It is time we regain respect and admiration for all of creation and see the beauty in nature's diversity.

Do you observe the ego playing a role in conservation today? I see it through our projection of guilt, blame, shame, and anger on all those we perceive as enemies to conservation. We make them wrong and evil and hope to punish them into compliance. I also see a lot of self-proclaimed conservation "heroes" today that receive much recognition and many accolades for being saviors of species and the environment. I see a large amount of greed contributing toward the loss of ecological integrity. And I see a plethora of corrupt politicians and officials, as well as a fair share of nonprofits with ill agendas.

Letting go of the ego means letting go of the need to be right, the need to win, the need for recognition, the need to control, and the need to judge. It is human nature to identify with our ego so we shouldn't judge ourselves for it. Rather, we can practice recognizing the ego in ourselves and in others as a means of minimizing its power over us.

Just having awareness of the ego is a great first step to raising your consciousness. Once you develop this awareness, you will tap into your true inner self more readily and the ego will lose its grip over your mind. This will allow you to channel your energy into effecting positive change for the greater good rather than wasting your energy worrying about what others are doing and remaining in a state of competition with them.

The inner self

The inner self is our inherent, divine, essential self. Our spirit. Whereas the ego is continually changing based on life experience, the inner self is a constant. It is directly connected to a higher power. It is who we are irrespective of personality, titles, and social identity. It is static and unchangeable. When we are connected with our soul, we are living in a state of awareness. We are tapped into our divine energy and to all of life itself. We live according to our inner voice, our intuition, our gut feelings. We feel guided beyond rational thought and connected deeply within ourselves as well as to the universe. Life often falls into place somewhat effortlessly and we begin to see the synchronicity of life rather than the obstacles and disappointments. We feel that people and events come into our lives for a reason. We lose judgment on whether things are good or bad. We focus on the lessons that life brings to us and recognize that our job is to learn the lessons so that life can continue to unfold. We live according to the guidance of our inner self and connect with our passion, which is our purpose. We exude our passion, our purpose, and our essence into the world as positive energy and inspire those around us. People are drawn to us rather inexplicably.

We have been programmed throughout our lives to live according to our egos, and it is unrealistic to think that this attachment can completely dissolve overnight. However, by simply bringing awareness to the thoughts in our minds and by becoming the observer of those thoughts, we can begin to tap into our inner self and thus our inner power. The more we practice being aware of our thoughts, the easier it becomes. We then begin to recognize that most of the thoughts in our head are useless, whether they be negative or repetitive or simply noise to fill the silence. Our inner self exists in the space between thoughts.

The Ecocentric Approach

We need more eco and less ego. Conscious conservation adopts an ecofocused approach to leadership. As a result, individuals tap into their inner selves rather than their egos and use this to guide their thoughts, feelings, actions, and outcomes. The individual recognizes the power within. They recognize that their inner state is reflected in their outer world. They adopt a universal system of values, as opposed to a self-centered one. Additionally, by placing humans firmly into the ecological equation, the ecocentric approach is inclusive of humans as a necessary component to achieve a return to balance.

To shift into an ecocentric approach to conscious conservation:

- Listen to your inner self and intuition as a guide for achieving the greater good for conservation (vs the ego)
- Have the goal of ecological balance in mind (vs personal agenda or motives in favor of one species or a singular component of conservation)
- Work as a steward of the planet to foster healing through a mindset of embodiment (rather than by fixing and "doing") and thus inspire others and lead by example

Mother Nature is inherently resilient. If we focus on a return to balance and make space for healing, she is capable of restoration. In order to facilitate this, we must adopt a more ecocentric approach, rather than an egocentric one.

Summary

Takeaways

- When ego dominates, the focus shifts from working toward the greater good, or for biodiversity preservation and restoring ecological balance, to winning, recognition, success, and being seen as a hero
- The ecocentric approach taps into the inner self, strives for ecological balance, and seeks to inspire others

Questions for reflection

1. In what ways have you allowed your ego to lead you in conservation?
2. Can you think of examples where the ego plays a role in conservation? Where in order for one to be right or to win in conservation someone must then be in the wrong or a loser?

Less doing, more being

The ego drives us to "do," as it gathers its worth based on our achievements in this world. Our inner self is the essence of "being." Our true worth is not based on what we do but who we are and how we show up in the world. The eco-mindset is focused on improving oneself in order to inspire others, rather than on changing others and labeling them as the "problem."

To help facilitate your inner transformation, it is extremely beneficial to meditate. Spending time in meditation helps us explore and uncover our inner source of life, energy, and connection to the universe. Research shows that meditation takes us out of our self-centered approach to life and brings us into a perspective of clarity and reverence for all life.[8] You will become the observer of your thoughts and recognize that you are the awareness behind the thoughts. This will help you to recognize when the ego is the driving force behind your decisions, or when the ego is responsible for negative talk or doubts.

This recognition helps to minimize the ego's choke hold over your actions. It will also help you recognize when your colleagues or peers are letting their ego get in the way of their focus on conservation.

Have a sense of humor about this—it is challenging for us to completely let go of our ego. However we can minimize its influence in our work simply by recognizing its presence and not taking it too seriously, whether in ourselves or in others.

THE COMPASSIONATE WARRIOR

he true soldier fights not because he hates what is in front of him, but because he loves what is behind him.

~G.K. Chesterton

The Endless Cycle

What happens when we hear about the senseless killing of iconic wildlife? We demonize the poacher, spew hatred online, and express our desire to kill or torture the poachers, crying out for vigilante justice. When the dust settles, the atrocity has not been erased. The animal or someone who devoted their life to protecting them is dead. Many times the perpetrators will walk free, and we are left feeling outraged, angry, sad, or frustrated. We express our displeasure on social media, but is that measurably productive? It may bring about a modest amount of success in terms of raising awareness and support for effecting change, but it falls short of generating sustainable change or helping us process and move forward. Rather than process and release these difficult emotions, we allow them to fester by ruminating on them, which causes an endless monologue of negativity in our minds. We use these negative thoughts as fuel to continue the fight. And so the "war" persists, and daily we are met with news of continued brutality and destruction. This compounds our anger and we begin to feel helpless, fearing we will never be able to stop the carnage.

As time goes on, a sense of hopelessness sets in and there is a loss of trust in the system, which has failed us. This strengthens our "us against them" mentality as we feel pitted against our foes—poachers and criminal syndicates, corrupt governments and officials, politicians, and the uncaring citizens of the world.

All of this can lead us into a victim mentality that places blame on the rest of the world and frees us from the responsibility of solving the problems we see. We feel as if the atrocities of the world are happening to us, and it is deeply painful to experience. We become too busy placing blame to consider an alternative viewpoint, a new perspective, or to create sustainable solutions. We must be willing to stop participating in the blame game in order to move beyond the crisis.

The conservation world is rife with corruption, greed, ill-intent, and at times even pure evil. Make no mistake, you have every right to feel outraged, angry, and, yes, helpless at times. Staying stuck in these emotions, however, does no one any good and does nothing to transform conservation challenges.

The Problem with Conservation Wars

War and transformation cannot coexist simultaneously. Conflict and war with another engages a part of your primitive brain known as the amygdala. The focus is on survival. You cannot have simultaneous focus on transformation and survival. When you are in survival mode, it is all-consuming, and all energy is directed to the fight for life. You cannot be in a relaxed, creative, healing state when in this mode. Thus when we adopt the mindset of being "at war," we stay stuck in a primitive survival mode rather than progressing forward toward growth and transformation.

So long as we fight poaching with an unconscious approach, we will never stop it. For every poacher we deter, there will be a dozen more to take their place. There will still be winners and losers. It becomes only a matter of time before the next battle erupts. This is not sustainable in the long term. We all must find a way to coexist on this planet. We are like a diseased body with all our resources spent in the acute phase of the illness, scrambling in the fight against poaching. If we continue at this rate, we will become chronically fatigued and suffer a breakdown before we have a chance to remedy the situation. We must allocate some of our collective resources, innovation, creativity, and knowledge in areas complementary to the frontline battle so that we may tackle the challenge in a more comprehensive manner. We are immersed in the moment-to-moment battle mentality of survival. Where we choose to go from here will determine the outcome. We can force this "disease" to merely go dormant, below the surface but still viable and reproducing, ready to erupt given the right environmental stressors. Or we can treat the disease at the root cause by applying conscious conservation.

The Angry Warrior versus the Compassionate Warrior

Are you leading yourself and others from a place of power or from force? Are you leading from a place of peace, compassion, and love, or are you leading from a place of frustration, anger, and revenge? Indeed it is necessary to deter, detain, and pursue justice (legal judgment and punishment) for those who attempt to harm Mother Nature or her guardians, and it is necessary to protect and defend the defenseless. But if you are doing so from a place of frustration, anger, and revenge, you are reliant upon the energy of force, which is much weaker than the energy of power. You are being controlled and guided by your anger. This is a position of weakness, as you are at the mercy of your negative emotions. We should not desire nor seek to carry out acts of violence on humans in the name of protecting and defending wildlife. It may be a necessary consequence of defending the defenseless, but should never be sought after. Peace must be a state of mind before it can be witnessed in the world around you. It begins with a peaceful heart. Set your intention for peace and your actions will follow suit.

Conservation warriors are plentiful these days. They can be found anywhere from the front lines of the fight against illegal harvesting of wildlife and protected species to lobbying for policy change and advocating for change via social media. But are you an angry warrior or a compassionate warrior? It is a critical distinction to make. Let's have a look at the two very different types of conservation warriors.

The angry warrior has a keen sense of what is right and what is wrong, and they use this moral compass to guide and shape their world view. The compassionate warrior upholds what they know in their heart to be true, as the knowledge of truth comes from the heart. It is an unspoken awareness also known as life force, spirit, universal truth, or God. Because they identify with this universal truth, they needn't judge circumstances as right or wrong, good or bad, as these are labels used by the ego, and they provide a false sense of reality and a false sense of strength, confidence, and righteousness.

The goal of the angry warrior is to bring justice to the world, based on their views of right and wrong. They execute this justice through forceful means of cooperation that include retribution, payback (incorrectly called karma), teaching the bad guys a lesson, blame, shame, and winning. The goal of the compassionate warrior is to bring compassion to the world based on the compassion they know within. They do not wish to right the wrongs or to punish, blame, or shame. They do not wish to harm another or to cause suffering. They seek legal justice rather than vigilante justice. They seek resolution to the challenge and a restoration of balance by transforming those whose actions are harmful to conservation.

The angry warrior has hatred and disgust for those who destroy Mother Nature and uses this disgust to fuel their actions to right the wrongs committed. The compassionate warrior condemns the actions of those who harm Mother Nature and her guardians rather than condemn the person responsible. The compassionate warrior still experiences sadness, frustration, anger, and disappointment, but they process and release these feelings in order to return to a state of peace. They know that feelings, if repressed or suppressed, will only serve as poison that destroys from within.

The angry warrior works through force to coerce, convince, intimidate, and overpower others to change. The compassionate warrior operates through power to inspire and empower others to change.

The angry warrior carries the intention to win, be right, or to punish the perceived villain. The compassionate warrior carries the intention to create transformation. The key distinction here is the inner driver of the outcome. The outcome may be the same in terms of what is necessary to protect and defend the defenseless. The motivator however is vastly different.

Some may argue that we should fight with the spirit of anger in our hearts to energize us and keep us motivated to demand change. Yet fighting with anger or negativity in our hearts is like drinking poison and expecting the other person to die. We are the only ones who suffer. Anger is a toxin that drains us and distracts us from connecting with our divine, true power. Our energy is wasted on managing and recycling the negative emotions inside. Fighting with negative emotions is a forceful way to demand the respect we desire. It is nowhere near as effective, or sustainable, as a compassionate heart.

The compassionate warrior always chooses love over fear. Remember that fear and sadness are often hiding underneath anger. The compassionate warrior protects their heart, as it is the greatest weapon in their arsenal.

Compassion is more powerful than anger. It is one of the most powerful forces in the universe.

Fighting from a place of negativity reflects a desire to control another in order for us to obtain the results we desire. If the "enemy" will do XYZ, we will be satisfied. The world will be right. We will win. This approach is tenuous at best. We may succeed in controlling the actions of another for the time being, but there will be a transference of negative emotions from us to the ones we are controlling, and they will now become frustrated, angry, or fearful. This is not a sustainable approach, as the fire of resentment will build and can erupt again at any time. They may adopt the psychology of rebellion and resist compliance at some point. It also does nothing to address the root cause that motivated their actions in the first place. Thus we are never truly free from the threat of recurrence and must either continue to exert control to receive compliance or risk a backlash.

Are there areas of your work as a conservationist where you are allowing the angry warrior to take over, thus diminishing your power? Are you demanding change through force or inspiring change through power? We must have the willingness to protect all beings who do not have a voice. This is an essential component of every conservationist. We may all have an innate desire to do so. The critical difference is whether we are doing so with a poisoned heart or a compassionate one. Believe in your voice, but use it wisely, calmly, and with conviction.

Which type of conservation warrior are you?

Summary

Takeaways

The angry warrior:

- Lives in a state of heightened alert or warrior mode (this fight-or-flight state is both physiologically and energetically taxing)
- Takes a defensive stance on conservation challenges and is ready to argue or fight their position as right, thus labeling others as wrong
- Lives in survival mode; engages the primitive brain (amygdala)
- Has a narrow viewpoint; focuses on short-term tactics
- Is determined to win (thus someone will lose)

- Achieves objectives through force (restriction, fighting, compliance, fear tactics)
- Seeks revenge on conservation foes
- Uses negative emotions such as frustration, anger, hatred, or disgust to fuel their actions

The compassionate warrior:

- Returns to a state of homeostasis after emotional upset; lives mostly in a parasympathetic or relaxed state where creativity and productivity thrive
- Takes an open-minded stance or outlook on circumstances related to conservation and is ready to listen and understand all sides of the challenge; does not place labels of right and wrong
- Lives in a state of awareness and observation; engages the frontal cortex
- Has a broad viewpoint; focused on long-term solutions
- Is determined to transform challenges and find solutions that work best for all
- Achieves objectives through power (alternatives, compassion, innovation, empowerment)
- Seeks resolution with conservation foes
- Uses awareness, intuition, and compassion to fuel their actions

Questions for reflection

1. Take a look around you—can you distinguish between the angry and the compassionate warriors in conservation?
2. Are you an angry warrior or a compassionate warrior?

Less doing, more being

Focus less on fighting arguing, hating, revenge, retribution, justice, and taking control, and more on developing compassion for all sides of the issue. Become the peace inside that you wish to see and inspire others from a position of power rather than force. Compassion is a powerful state of being that can bring about positive transformation not only for the person who becomes compassionate, but for those who receive compassion as well.

Seek to find common ground with conservation foes, so you can dissolve the divide and foster more empathy for their circumstances and behaviors. "Being" requires an extension of empathy toward those we previously judged and an understanding of their position and their pain. As you encounter difficult circumstances, protect your mental and emotional health by processing and releasing negative emotions, rather than stuffing them away or trying to reason your way through them.

Practice forgiveness, as it will set you free from the burden of carrying around negative or toxic emotions that weigh you down and drain your energy. Facilitate and inspire change by applying compassion to the challenges you see, rather than attempting to force change through contempt.

COMPASSIONATE CONSERVATION

ove and compassion are necessities, not luxuries. Without them, humanity cannot survive.

~ *Dalai Lama XIV, The Art of Happiness*

Compassion in Conservation

Compassion is a desire to understand the behaviors, motivations, and emotions of another being. It is an extension of empathy, as it comprises a desire to alleviate the suffering of that being. Compassion is an essential component of conscious conservation and can be applied to all aspects of conservation in action. It can be applied through our actions:

- Toward wildlife
- Toward the earth and its ecosystems
- Toward ourselves
- Toward human communities at the interface
- Toward one another—our colleagues and peers, as well as our foes

Toward wildlife

This may seem rather obvious, and is perhaps the easiest one to practice, as a love of all things wild is inherent in most all conservationists. However, conservation hasn't historically applied compassion to its regard and treatment of wildlife. It is therefore worth mentioning in order to remind ourselves that wildlife are sentient beings capable of feelings such as joy and pain. Sadly, much of the chronic pain experienced by wildlife is due to our own carelessness or cruelty. So long as there is imbalance in this way, and there are humans on this earth who do not feel compassion toward all beings, it is our duty to teach compassion, and to do so by example. This is not the same as preaching compassion. Preaching often falls on deaf ears as it leaves others feeling judged and inferior. Teach through your actions and you will inspire others to adopt a similar outlook.

We cannot save all beings. The planet can only support a limited supply of life on earth. However it is our duty to extend care and compassion and to assist animals in need and, anytime their suffering is of human origin, it is our duty to intervene. If an animal is injured through natural (non-human-induced) causes, unless the animal is suffering greatly, wildlife veterinarians typically do not intervene. The exception to this rule is for threatened, endangered, or nationally protected species.

Toward the earth and its ecosystems

Compassion toward the earth includes actions that support a return to a more balanced state. We have enormous power as citizens of the earth, and as conservationists, to enact change through our everyday actions. As buyers we have the power to choose products that are ethically sourced, fairly traded, and environmentally friendly. We can directly support companies who do the same and discontinue buying products from companies who are environmentally unfriendly. We can live a life that is gentler on the environment, starting with our ecological footprint. Many of these ideas are well circulated, such as recycling, energy efficiency, minimalism, and the like. These actions absolutely make a difference in supporting environmental health, biodiversity, and the restoration of ecological balance globally.

Toward ourselves

We must extend compassion to ourselves, as it is from within that we will draw the energy and strength to change the world around us. We must learn to practice self- care, as it is critical for good health. We will not inspire others and foster change if we are frustrated and exhausted by modern conservation issues, nor if we are overly stressed or overworked. We must extend patience to ourselves and extend compassion to our imperfections.

When we do the inner work to clear space for more optimism in conservation, we will see the world around us respond in kind.

Toward human communities at the interface

We must extend compassion to all those who live in conflict with wildlife and to those who are more directly dependent on natural resources than we are in the developed world. We cannot pretend to fully understand what it is like to have our entire year's supply of food wiped out in one night by roaming elephants or to have a loved one killed by a tiger. It is only when we develop empathy for those living at the interface with wildlife and protected habitats that we can begin to understand their motivations and behaviors. If we wish to support a return to balance, ecological health, and the preservation of wildlife and wild spaces, we must focus on the interface and support the people living "at the edge."

You cannot remedy anything by condemning it. ~ Wayne Dyer.

Toward one another—our colleagues and peers, as well as our foes

It is here we may find the most difficulty, extending compassion to those we believe to be harming the earth, wild spaces, or wildlife in some way, whether directly or indirectly. Why should we extend compassion to these people who commit heinous crimes and destroy what we love and cherish?

By holding contempt for them, or any negative emotions such as hate, frustration, anger, or disgust, we are lowering our own energy and wasting it, taking it away from our efforts to make positive change in the world. We give away our power to them, making their actions even more potent. Our negative emotions do nothing to change them.

Holding contempt does however change us for the worse.

Framing them as an enemy or villain makes them the problem and thus separate from the ecological equation we wish to protect. It is critical to understand that they are a part of the environment, whether we choose to accept this or not. They live on the earth and have a relationship of give and take, whether good or bad. Until we remove those labels, we block our own ability to see possibility in the challenge.

By labeling and separating good and bad humans, we are operating from a place of control. This gives our power away and places it in the hands of those we have labeled as bad. It also uses control to try and force compliance. Asking them to conform is not an effective way of creating lasting, sustainable change.

By removing labels and working to extend compassion to those we previously labeled as bad, we can influence their behavior through the most powerful of all emotions, that of compassion, rather than through forcing them to adhere to a set of rules that only we may fully understand. By understanding their perspective and pain points, we open ourselves to creative solutions that benefit the people we once labeled as the problem while preserving wildlife and wild spaces at the same time. This may additionally help create more economic value in nature.

We must find common ground with our foes in order to dissolve the divide.

Unfortunately, there will always be negative, bad, and terrible happenings in the world. Humans will continue to commit unspeakable acts in the name of greed. Focusing on this magnifies it. If we don't move through the pain and into compassion, we will remain stuck in the pain of the circumstance and transform the pain into suffering. This isn't to say we shouldn't pay respect to terrible events. Rather, we shouldn't dwell on them and refuse to release the emotions, turning them into chronic suffering. We then become trapped as victims of the pain.

The Evolution

Cultivating a compassionate approach to conservation requires us to shift our mindset. It requires an inner transformation that leads to a transformation of the world around us.

This shift takes place as an evolution from unconscious to conscious perception. As unconscious conservationists, we feel that conservation challenges happen *to* us, or *against* us. Our perception is based upon resistance, reaction, and a defensive viewpoint. The egoic mind predominates. We have a victim mentality whereby we feel personally hurt and attacked by ecological destruction, or an angry warrior mentality where we must fight to prevent the destruction. It is a feeling of helplessness and negative emotion toward our perceived foes. As conscious conservationists we understand that conservation challenges happen *for* us. If we look within the challenge we will find a blueprint for what must be done to transform the challenge in order to remedy it. This is a shift in perception. We understand the lessons are here to teach us. There is a surrendering to what is and acceptance of things as they are. This opens the possibility to see the opportunity within the challenge and to grow and transform both ourselves as individuals as well as the challenge itself.

Unconscious conservationists believe in a "doing" model of conservation whereby, to bring about change, we must change others who are perceived as conservation foes, as wrong, or as evil. Thus it is action from a position of force rather than power. Conscious conservationists make the connection between the transformation within and how it is reflected without. It is recognized that our perception is our reality, and that suffering comes from the thoughts we think, whether through projecting the past into the present or worrying about the future and projecting that anxiety into the present. Awareness begins to develop and circumstances can be viewed as they are, without labels or judgment. There is now more clarity and thus more creation of innovative solutions. Finally, we become the embodiment of conservation itself. We have now become that which we wish to see in the world. We are the embodiment of balance, of compassion and peace. Countless others are influenced and inspired through our example. Conscious conservation is practiced in order to transform challenges into opportunities.

Summary

Takeaways

To be a compassionate conservationist is to:

- Take action that prevents or relieves the suffering of wildlife
- Take action that preserves ecological integrity and/or is not at the expense of ecological integrity
- Foster self-care and avoid compassion fatigue, burnout, and a negative mindset
- Take action that mitigates human-wildlife conflict and demonstrates care and concern for the welfare and well-being of communities in conflict with wildlife or lacking access to adequate resources
- Dissolve the zero-sum mentality that results in conservation foes

Questions for reflection

1. In what areas of conservation could you apply compassion in order to transform the situation from a challenge into an opportunity?
2. Do you feel emotionally victimized by the conservation challenges you face? How can you transform your mindset to

view these challenges as opportunities for growth as a conservationist, and for transformation of current practices?

3. Do you believe that conservation challenges happen *to* you, or *against* you, rather than *for* you, as an opportunity for learning and a blueprint for transformation? How can you transform your mindset to view yourself as the embodiment of what you wish to see in conservation?

Less doing, more being

In unconscious conservation, we spend our time "doing" things in order to attempt to control or change that which we do not like or that which is undesirable.

Conscious conservation is more about a state of becoming that which we wish to see in the world. It is about a state of being. Compassion in conservation includes compassion toward all beings, including reserving judgment against humans whose actions are damaging toward conservation. Being compassionate helps dissolve the barriers that divide us, as we begin to understand and empathize with the needs and motivations of those we disagree with. We stop allowing the bad in the world to dictate our ability to do good. This allows us to find solutions that benefit both sides, thus dissolving the challenge. Cultivating compassion begins with an extension of compassion to ourself. Focus on practicing gratitude rather than focusing on the negative. Extend compassion to yourself by being kinder and more forgiving of your flaws or shortcomings. From here you can begin to work on extending compassion to those you have judged harshly as conservation foes.

Examine the areas of conservation where a more compassionate approach can be applied. For example, rather than only viewing the facts and statistics surrounding conservation challenges, take time to understand the stories behind the challenge. Identify the inhumanity of our greatest conservation challenges and apply humanity to transform the challenge.

PART IV
A SHIFT IN APPROACH

Now that we have shifted our point of view and our mindset, it is time to bring to life these inner transformations by shifting our approach to conservation. It begins with including humans in the ecological equation and inspiring others through providing information rather than instilling fear or anger through sensationalism. Next we will examine how to uncover the root causes of the conservation challenges we face today. Finally, we will combine scientific knowledge with our own internal compass and use an intuitive approach to conservation.

SOLVING HUMAN-BASED PROBLEMS

*W**hen one tugs at a single thing in nature, he finds it attached to the rest of the world.*

~John Muir

Human Conservation

We must be willing to listen to the needs and problems of the people living at the interface with the wildlife we hope to protect if we are ever going to have a chance to save the wildlife. If we hope to help wildlife, we must first help the people. In essence, we must retrain ourselves to have compassion for humanity and learn to focus on humans as a critical species of importance to the future of conservation globally. Conservation should not imply saving one species to the detriment of another. Nor can we save all individuals of a species. Rather, conservation strives to achieve and sustain ecological health and ecological balance and to preserve biodiversity.

When we include humans in the ecological equation, it is clear that we are out of balance and our population has become too large for long-term sustainability. As a result, we see more disease outbreaks among humans as well as at the interface between humans, domestic animals, and wildlife. We also see increasing competition for resources and increasing anthropogenic stressors on Mother Nature. We have reached a tipping point. If we do not learn the lessons in time, we will see catastrophic effects. By focusing on the challenges humans are facing in modern times, especially in the developing world where humans live in close contact with nature and wildlife, we will alleviate some of the anthropogenic stressors driving our conservation crises.

Empower humans within the challenge to become part of the solution

Once we reinsert ourselves into the ecological equation, we become part of that which we wish to preserve. We have an inherent investment in biodiversity preservation, as nature is seen as a direct extension of us, and we are seen as part of nature. Rather than preaching to others about practicing conservation because it is the right thing to do, we educate and demonstrate how it contributes to human health, human livelihoods, and well-being. We show others that by preserving biodiversity, they are contributing directly to their health and that of their families, their communities, and future generations. We must instill into conservationists as well as the younger generation the desire to reinvest in humanity. We must inspire and train new conservationists who are willing to focus first and foremost on the human species. We must redefine what it means to be a conservationist.

It is true that humans are responsible for the majority of the challenges we face as modern conservationists. However, it is largely a result of removing ourselves from the ecological equation in the first place.

We cannot hope to achieve positive results through reprimanding, punishing, restricting, arguing, persuading, begging, and demanding that people comply with conservation policies if they don't have a personal investment in the system to begin with. This forceful approach is a temporary fix at best. The successful approach involves empowering people to recognize their interdependent relationship with nature. Truly, what we do to nature, we do to ourselves.

Once we begin to view human beings as an intricate part of the ecosystem, we have the opportunity to bring human populations, along with our habits and behaviors, back into ecological balance. Once balance is restored, nature has a miraculous way of healing herself. We can facilitate this healing by shifting the focus of conservation toward the mitigation of humanity's ecologically destructive impacts.

The future of conservation lies in the ability not only to integrate the human species into an ecological framework, but also to develop means for humans to become part of the solution rather than "the problem." This shift will empower humans to take ownership in their role as a dynamic part of the ecosystem, eliminating the need to blame and shame them. Empowering humans encourages sustainability and creates a ripple effect, as those who are empowered lead by example and thus empower others.

This is the conscious approach to conservation.

Community-Based Conservation

In conservation there are geographical regions that are hotspots of activity between humans, domestic animals, wildlife, and their environment. This interaction can be seen as an interdependency, as the actions of one have direct and indirect impacts on the others. Thus interactions such as subsistence hunting for food or trade, human-wildlife conflict, disease transmission, and deforestation due to land-use change all take place at what we refer to in conservation as the interface. The developing world has a higher degree of interface, thus communities in the developing world are in a "frontline" position both to implement and benefit from conservation initiatives. This is known as community-based conservation.

Historically, and even in present day, conservation has been more of an exclusionary practice, with the power of decision-making belonging to people of wealth, influence, or status. The future of conservation must include close collaboration with communities at the dynamic interface with nature. Community-based conservation is the way forward. It is of the people, by the people, and for the people.

Community-based conservation:

- Is an inclusive approach
- Is reliant upon relationship-building and trust
- Includes the roles of women in the community, with efforts to educate and empower them
- Integrates closely with social sciences, as an understanding of the psychology of humans is crucial to the success of community-based initiatives
- Is a bottom-up approach, with engagement of the community's wants and needs throughout the decision-making process

- Is a "can do" approach versus a "can't do" approach (less authoritarian, less restriction and policing of the people)
- Relies on the wisdom, knowledge, and experience of people at the interface to develop culturally appropriate, sustainable solutions

Apply cultural context to solutions

The transdisciplinary approach to conservation combines a multidisciplinary approach with a close collaboration between conservationists and communities directly impacted by conservation challenges. It engages those most affected by the issues during each step of the remediation process. By engaging with community members adjacent to or part of the wild spaces we wish to preserve, we develop an understanding of their needs and wants. When we incorporate their ideas, needs, and wants into each step of the process, culturally relevant solutions are created by community members themselves, and challenges unique to the community are addressed. This approach increases compliance and thus success, as we are no longer imposing our own ideas, suggestions, values, and demands on the community. We are instead facilitating and empowering them to problem-solve according to their own priorities and cultural context. The transdisciplinary approach is a means to empower locals to engage in the conservation process to develop solutions that are sustainable and balanced. We introduce the idea that human beings are part of the ecosystem and thus help people to understand their place ecologically so they can problem- solve from this perspective.

The psychology of "can't do"

When we demand that humans stop engaging in certain behaviors that are considered to be detrimental ecologically without providing them a reasonable alternative, resentment and rebellion typically ensue. This is known as reactance in psychology, and it is a behavioral response to rules or regulations that threaten to eliminate certain behavioral freedoms. Reactance occurs when someone feels that certain life choices are being taken away or restricted, with limitations placed on reasonable alternatives. This often occurs when people are pressured to adopt a certain viewpoint or attitude that isn't in concert with their behavior. Reactance increases resistance to the suggested change. It also increases the likelihood that individuals will engage in the prohibited activity or behavior in rebellion to the authority figure, regardless of risk or circumstance.[9]

Now that humans are included in the ecological equation, conservationists must develop an understanding of human psychology and behavior. Conservation should integrate with the social sciences, in particular with human psychology, sociology, and economics, in order to achieve sustainable, successful, long-term solutions to the challenges we face in conservation.

When we focus on telling people what they cannot do, without providing them reasonable alternatives that are ecologically sustainable, we cannot expect them to comply in the long run. Eventually these "can't do" tactics will fail. As conservationists, we must find and provide reasonable solutions to conservation challenges that are sustainable ecologically, as well as economically, psychologically, and sociologically.

By taking ownership as an ecologically integrated species, we embody the understanding that what we do to nature, we do to ourselves. This is a concept familiar to many conservationists, but not necessarily acknowledged by the entire human race. When we see ourselves as an integral part of the natural world, we will take more pride in our position as guardians of the ecosystem. We will be more cautious with the utilization of resources. We will begin to look at all members of our species not as enemies or villains, but instead as fellow beings that need guidance and inspiration rather than condemnation for their ecological contribution. If we continue trying to change others from a place of force through judgment, restriction, argument, and forced compliance to the rules and regulations, there will be resentment and rebellion.

Eventually this will lead to a failure of compliance. We can choose to inspire and motivate others to adopt a more harmonious lifestyle, not through compliance, but from a place of willingness.

Healthy planet, healthy people

Nature is a symphony, and every native species plays a unique and vital part ecologically. Historically, we have pillaged some species to extinction or to the very brink of extinction, and as a result, nature and her ecosystems are out of balance. Some species are overabundant, whether due to human preference for hunting, sport, or recreation, or because they are opportunistic species that thrive in a variety of conditions. Overpopulated wildlife species must be managed, while others are so scarce that drastic measures are necessary to ensure their survival. This creates an imbalanced approach to conservation, whereby we are scrambling to recreate a natural balance. Yet we cannot replicate what nature has perfected. What we can do is to place a focus on her masterpiece—ecological biodiversity—and facilitate the preservation of remaining biodiverse regions while working to restore areas that have lost their biodiversity and ecological balance. If we focus on biodiversity as the ultimate goal, species preservation will take place more readily as an element of the ultimate goal. Unfortunately, we must still work hard to preserve endangered species whose future remains on the line.

In order to better appreciate the importance of biodiversity, we must understand the ways in which humans benefit from healthy ecosystems, such as clean drinking water, nutrient recycling, food availability, and crop pollination. These benefits are known as ecosystem services. Humans don't just take from the ecosystem. We readily give back to the environment in positive and (mostly) negative ways. It is a dynamic interchange. We must convince people of the critical role that nature plays in the health and well-being of humanity. Our life, and that of all species, depends on it. Integrating conservation with public health will help to reinforce the link between human health and the health of the planet.

We must also find ways to value the living wild animal over that of its parts. For far too long, humans have treasured wildlife parts as commodities, whether it be for sport, for health, or for recreation. Until we find a way to value free-ranging wildlife over wildlife parts, we will continue to lose species and witness the suffering and killing of wildlife. Free-ranging wildlife must hold value for the communities of people who live at the interface. As conservationists, we must listen to the needs of the human species at the interface with wildlife and the environment and support them in finding sustainable ways to utilize natural resources. We must find ways for all of humanity to value natural resources and free-ranging wildlife for their importance in maintaining ecological health and well-being, which includes the health and well-being of humans. This is the key to our future success in conservation.

Summary

Takeaways

- As conservationists we should view humans as part of the ecological equation, and thus focus on solving human-based problems
- Empower humans within the challenge to become part of the solution
- Use a community-based, "can do" approach versus a "can't do" approach
- Value and promote the benefit of healthy ecosystems and biodiversity, and create value for living wildlife over their parts

Questions for reflection

1. How can you change your approach in conservation to include humans as a species of focus so that they are empowered and become part of the solution?
2. How can you collaborate with colleagues in complementary disciplines, in particular those related to human health, well-being, economics, and behavior, in order to enhance your work as a conservationist?
3. Is your overarching goal in conservation to restore ecological balance and preserve biodiversity?

Less doing, more being

Begin a dialogue with colleagues in complementary disciplines, including human psychology and behavior, economics, or politics and consider collaboration that will enhance your knowledge and understanding as it relates to your work in conservation. Consider the human side of the equation in conservation challenges and engage and empower those at the heart of the challenge with ways to transform it. Devise solutions that don't rely on specialists or a high investment or advanced technology, but rather engage and involve citizen conservationists and community members, allowing their input and action to transform the situation.

Create a message that inspires others to cherish ecological health and biodiversity, and share how it benefits humans as well. Be mindful of the long-term goal of restoring ecological health and resiliency, as well as that of biodiversity preservation, and determine how your short- term conservation efforts contribute to the big picture. Adjust your goals as needed in order to align them with a return to ecological balance.

INSPIRATIONAL CONSERVATION

hen we love, we always strive to become better than we are. When we strive to become better than we are, everything around us becomes better too. ~Paulo Coelho

Raising Awareness Versus Raising Consciousness

News and social media are rife with stories that highlight the incessant polluting of our oceans, the unrelenting conversion of native habitat for human use, the ruthless poaching of iconic wildlife, and the destruction of our planet. Regardless of whether we get the majority of our conservation news from social media, the news media, or academia, doom and gloom is all around us. The issue of loss is a predominant theme in conservation. A Google search for conservation news brings up plenty of "sky is falling" articles. Sensationalism sells in modern conservation. The media trend is to cherry-pick stories that are eye-catching, and the more horrific, shocking, frightening, or terrible, the better to garner readership. This sensationalism plays to our tendency to gravitate toward a negative bias, and the result is an overwhelming amount of negative news circulating in our world today. This holds true for conservation as well as for global ecological health. Social media provides a platform that has tremendous potential to influence and the power to effect change in conservation. Negative media keeps us triggered emotionally and distracts us from potential solutions. And it allows us to place blame on those we view as foes, resulting in a zero-sum game where we desire compliance through force in order to elicit change.

When we focus on the negative, we only see more negativity in our world. Perception is reality. What you focus on expands. Positive stories are more readily shared, and more likely to go viral, than those heavy with pessimism.[10] Thus if conservationists intend to raise awareness and create change, sharing stories about loss, devastation, and heartache may not only be ineffective, they may backfire, causing their potential audience to tune out and turn away, whether due to overwhelm, compassion fatigue, or sheer distaste of the content's tone. This is not to say we shouldn't educate others and share pertinent information. Rather there is a more effective way to educate and raise awareness, one that has nothing to do with doom and gloom. Conscious conservation utilizes a "conservation with inspiration" philosophy. We share information in a way that serves to empower and inspire people and compel them to act from a place of power rather than from a position of fear or force.

Promoting the "Fight" Mentality

Many conservationists, organizations, and citizens view themselves as warriors, fighters, and advocates for what is "right," as well as for change. Advocacy is necessary, however if we are demanding change through the emotional filter of anger, righteousness, and a lack of compassion, is it an effective means of creating sustainable change? What are the outcomes, both for the advocate as well as the recipients, not to mention for conservation? All too often the loser falls on the side of conservation, as there will always be someone with more money, power, and influence to sway funds away from protecting resources and utilize them to pillage instead. Or the losers may be those we have labeled as our conservation enemies, be they politicians, corrupt officials, big businessmen, or poachers. The true losers of course in this scenario are all beings, humans and the species we continue to lose.

The point here is not to say that you shouldn't have strong emotional reactions to the injustices of conservation. Factual information, albeit at times depressing, has its rightful place in the media. But does the heavy reliance on harsh language and graphic images translate to meaningful, sustainable, positive change at the root of the issue?

Unfortunately, negative marketing campaigns influence the public's perception that organizations will do anything to solicit donor money, and serve to increase public resentment towards the charity.[11] Research also supports that guilt-based campaigns cause individuals to respond by avoiding further guilt, thus turning away from the negative stimulus entirely.[12]

This is not conscious conservation.

The heightened awareness we are creating is merely a heightened state of fear, of anger, of frustration, and overwhelm. We are merely crying out that there is a problem. We are desperate for another way. We are hungry for an end to the suffering. Yet we continue to pick at the wound.

There is a better way.

We are all well aware. We don't necessarily need to raise more awareness. So how then do we move beyond raising awareness and into raising consciousness? How do we inspire rather than trigger? Through stories that emphasize the personal element, that explain what is being done to create a better circumstance, that emphasize the positive, and that focus on sustainability, hope, and optimism. These are more effective ways to engage the audience and to convert support into meaningful action.[13]

It is part of human nature to focus on the negative in life. It is theorized to be a result of our evolution, as the need to avoid danger was a critical survival skill for our early ancestors.[14] In conservation, therefore, we must be consciously aware of this tendency in order to rise above it. We must consciously choose to focus on the positive as a counterbalance to the negative so that the negative doesn't cloud our perception of reality.

In modern conservation, raising awareness occurs primarily via social media, and social media is a network based on connections. When we share information, we are sharing it primarily within our own social circles. Our social circles are biased toward similarity in thinking, cultural familiarity, global outlook, opinions, and beliefs. This serves to reinforce our "rightness" and boosts our ego because we feel we are correct in our point of view. This doesn't provide us much opportunity to engage in discussion with individuals who have different thinking, cultural biases, global outlooks, opinions, and beliefs from our own. We remain blind to the "other side" and continue to have a myopic viewpoint regarding the challenges we face in conservation. Essentially, we are raising awareness among our peers who already think like we do. We aren't reaching out to those who may have distinctly different viewpoints. We also largely fail to reach those whom we may view as our conservation foes (politicians, corrupt officials, poachers, uncaring citizens). Thus we aren't raising the awareness of the very individuals we wish to influence. Additionally, our educational campaigns and organized protests rarely reach those we wish to influence or change. And when they do, unless it is an effective message that is culturally appropriate and seen to be of benefit or importance to their life and livelihood, it may be easily ignored or discarded. In essence, our message falls on deaf ears.

There is an urgent need for a more balanced approach to conservation news reporting. We must balance fear-mongering with stories of optimism and examples of innovative, successful, sustainable conservation. If our target audience is our supposed foes, in order to influence them we must first listen to understand their perspective, their pain points, and their motivations. We should focus on crafting our message in a way that is respectful, factual, and non-accusatory. We must find common ground with them if we ever hope to transform the situation from a negative to a positive. We must engage with communities at the interface in a way that is meaningful to them, and in a way that brings value to their life rather than detracts from it. In order for our efforts to be sustainable, we must empower those who currently exert a negative impact on conservation to change in a way that benefits them while also having a neutral or positive impact on conservation.

In order to raise awareness that leads to a measurable transformation of conservation's greatest challenges, we must begin to seek out that which we wish to become. Seek first those who inspire, rather than those who trigger. As we develop our own unique, more positive identity in conservation, we share it with those around us. We find that our positive outlook attracts more positive individuals and organizations into our life. We begin to inspire and be inspired. This is the beginning of elevating our consciousness. Surrounding ourselves with peers that take the conscious approach to conservation will help to inspire us to focus on the possibilities. And we in turn will serve as a source of inspiration to others. Your vibe attracts your tribe. Which would you rather associate with—those who trigger you emotionally or those who inspire you?

Compassion Fatigue and Distanciation

Compassion fatigue is defined twofold: firstly, as indifference to charitable appeals on behalf of those who are suffering, experienced as a result of the frequency or number of such appeals; secondly, as an extreme state of tension and preoccupation with the suffering of others experienced by those helping people or animals in distress.

Research shows that as numbers of victims increase, so does compassion fatigue.[15] This is a rather dismaying truth of human behavior, which seems to indicate that when individuals become statistics, it distances us from the ability to feel sympathy or compassion, the very emotions that compel us to act. Additionally it has a cumulative effect whereas over time we begin to feel numb to an emotional reaction from media images and stories that once elicited a response.[16] This is also known as distanciation.

Compassion fatigue doesn't discriminate, and it can impact anyone, from those working on the front lines of conservation to donors and supporters of conservation efforts. It is a coping mechanism that prevents us from going into complete overwhelm and shutdown. In order to cope or survive, one must develop some sense of distance from the story, lest it leave a more permanent scar.

Additionally, the barrage of depressing news is draining on those who truly care about the state of things. One cannot operate from a place of inspiration and power to effect positive change if they are emotionally triggered and busy reacting to fear, heartache, or hopelessness.

Over time, compassion fatigue leads to feelings of helplessness, followed by hopelessness. Helplessness is a feeling that our hands are tied, and that the problem is insurmountable or simply too big for us to make a difference. Hopelessness dictates that regardless of what is done, the fate is sealed and we are doomed to fail. A person then becomes bitter, resentful, and resigned to this fate. If we are without hope then we are without life itself. Thus we must work to avoid compassion fatigue and its sequelae of helplessness and hopelessness.

So how to keep hope alive in the face of so much bad news? The truth is, there are many bad trends today in conservation that are likely on a trajectory that won't stop overnight. We must be prepared to withstand more damage in the coming years. It likely will get much worse before it gets better. We do not control life's external forces. We do not control what happens in the world around us. We do however have absolute control over our internal world. And this is where our hope lives, grows, and is born again in the face of calamity. Hope, life, and love live within us. Thus we must look within if we wish to find hope for the future of conservation.

We as conservationists are the voice for the voiceless, the inspiration for positive change, but how can we possibly expect to influence others if we are stuck in the negativity trap and don't believe in it ourselves? Moreover we are discouraging our supporters, in particular the younger generation, from believing that they alone can make a measurable impact on conservation, further damning ourselves to accelerate the timeline to global destruction.

On a grander scale, how do we influence the flavor of stories that the news and social media feeds us? By ceasing to follow sensationalist stories or news outlets/social media/organizations that circulate stories in order to elicit an emotional reaction. By becoming discerning observers of the media we read or listen to and determining whether the story has logical information and a balanced approach, or whether it may be trying to manipulate us into an emotional reaction. By voicing our opinions and letting organizations we support know that we would love to hear more positive, inspirational stories and by using positive reinforcement to encourage them when they do so (if they have none to share, this is a red flag). And as conservationists, by creating stories that emphasize conservation successes equally as much, and I would argue more so, than conservation failures.

Coercion Versus Inspiration

Many organizations who rely on donor support fear that by focusing on their successes, they may alienate themselves from additional donor support. They become reliant upon the "sky is falling" approach in order to incite fear and panic in their donors, thereby forcing them to donate in order to keep the crisis from unfolding. Thus sensationalism sells for nonprofits just as it does for the media. No one likes to feel helpless and angry, yet this is what we tend to rely on with a preponderance of modern conservation's marketing schemes.

Consider two ways to inform your audience:

-Scenario one: we flood them with graphic images of poached wildlife, the number being killed daily, and how quickly we are losing remaining iconic species globally.

This overwhelms the receiver and they feel anger, sadness, fear, and hopelessness. They are not provided information on what they can do, and there is no call to action. They reply to our post with an emotional cry for help and change. They may share the post, but the magnitude of the issue is such that they feel as if their ability to donate a small amount of their time, tithe, or talent would not be sufficient to make a difference. In addition to feeling helpless about the cause, we have successfully made them feel helpless about their own ability to contribute in a meaningful way.

This form of news sharing typically serves to boost the ego of the messenger, as they are recognized for being the source of breaking news, and it elicits a large and heated response from the audience, making them feel important.

-Scenario two: we provide our audience with specific information on the issue of poaching as it relates to the trade in wildlife parts, as well as a few suggestions on actionable ways to contribute to our cause. This call to action may include small and reasonable contributions of time, talents, or tithing. One suggestion includes a request for ideas on how technology can assist in combatting the illegal wildlife trade.

It is likely that one person, one NGO, or one institution cannot stop the problem in its entirety. However one person, one organization, or one institution can devise an innovative solution that contributes to a comprehensive solution to the challenge. Take the Wildlife Crime Technology Challenge, an initiative issued by USAID and its partners as an effort to elicit innovative technology that can contribute to the fight against wildlife crime. In 2015 they requested submissions for technology that contributed to either the detection of transit routes, the strengthening of forensic evidence, the reduction of consumer demand, or the tackling of corruption, and received over 300 applications. Sixteen winners were chosen in all categories, providing a plethora of innovative technological solutions to help tackle the problem of wildlife crime, including ivory poaching.[17] This alone won't solve the problem of elephant population declines across the African continent, or the poaching of species like rhinos or pangolins, however it illustrates how individuals and individual organizations have the power and ability to contribute to the cause in significant ways.

Imagine the impact of hundreds of individuals each working toward a solution based on their own unique passion and abilities. Do you intend to overwhelm and frustrate your audience, rendering them incapable of contributing due to the seeming enormity of the problem, or do you intend to inspire and empower your audience by encouraging them to contribute in unique and meaningful ways?

We are the media. What we say matters. We have tremendous potential to influence others and to create change. Are you using social media to force your message or to empower others through your message? Are you using social media to condemn and project frustration, sadness, and hatred? Or are you using social media to support and inspire others?

Summary

Takeaways

- News and social media have become platforms for reinforcing

the negative rather than emphasizing and celebrating the positive stories of conservation
- Seek to inspire rather than use fear-based doom and gloom
- We are the media; use our influence for the greater good

Questions for reflection

1. In what areas of conservation do you see a preponderance of negativity?
2. Do you feel overwhelmed, helpless, or hopeless regarding conservation, or are you inspired by the information you receive through news and social media?
3. Are you using fear tactics to motivate others to action, or are you using inspiration?

Less doing, more being

Work on reacting less and relying on the reactions of others to create change, and instead take more action from a place of inspiration. When we react to the doom and gloom media that is designed to trigger a negative emotional response, we waste energy and do nothing to inspire others around us to act, other than in an equally negative way. We cannot implement true positive change from a negative mindset. Surround yourself with likeminded and positive people. Be mindful of the media you consume, as well as the media you create. Craft your message with a call to action that inspires others. If your job is to share unfortunate news, be mindful that your messages aren't intended to shock or scare, but rather to inform. Consider what you present to others through your words and actions —do you serve as an inspiration for positive change?

THE DEEP DIVE

*othing ever goes away until it has taught us what we need
to know.*

~Pema Chodron

Sinks and Sources

When a livestock-attacking lion is removed from its territory, a void
is created ecologically, also known as a sink. A new lion from a
neighboring source population will migrate in and claim this
territory. Thus a niche is created and then filled from the neighboring
supply population. In ecology this is referred to as source-sink
dynamics. We see a similar phenomenon in conservation with respect
to our ecologically destructive foes. For every poacher we arrest, there
are several more that fill the void. For every corrupt government
official removed, there is another one to take their place. For every
money-hungry business we stop from environmentally unsound
practices, there are endless more contributing to the challenge. This
occurs because we are targeting the issue at a superficial layer rather
than diving deeper into the root cause of the issue. When we focus on

the superficial cause rather than the root issue, we can never truly cure the disease. Thus we engage in an endless game of cat and mouse and expend precious energy and resources chasing after the "bad guys."

We must absolutely do what is necessary in the name of conservation to stop crime, corruption, and unethical behavior. We can go further than our current strategies however. We can and must dive deeper into the heart of the challenges we face. With poaching, demand reduction is absolutely necessary and will go a long way toward stopping the poaching crisis for the trade in wildlife parts. But demand reduction isn't the only root cause. We must also focus on ways to prevent future generations from choosing behaviors that are unsustainable and ecologically destructive in the first place. And we must fortify communities at the interface with wildlife such that there is no temptation to destroy natural resources in the name of survival or greed. We must raise the inherent value of nature for communities at the interface so that the value of free-ranging wildlife is greater than that of dead wildlife.

To do this, we must first understand the cultural, economic, nutritional, occupational, and behavioral pain points of the communities who live at the interface with threatened or endangered wildlife. Once we understand their pain points, we can support them in finding culturally appropriate solutions to their own unique challenges that elevate their overall well-being, enhance their livelihood, and promote sustainable utilization of natural resources while preserving and protecting wildlife.

The Deep Dive

A good bit of modern conservation involves putting out fires and working against a ticking clock to do what we can to save species and preserve habitat before all hope is lost. This is a form of triage used in medicine that pertains to critical care and emergency situations, where the focus is on survival rather than the fine-tuning and finessing of health. In the triage approach, we remain at the more superficial levels of conservation. There is however another complementary approach that serves to go deeper, beyond the surface of the problems as we see them, to uncover the root cause of the challenges we face today. When we take time to do a "deep dive" into the issue and discover the root cause, we can apply conscious conservation to implement sustainable success.

This is where the power of awareness comes in. We put on our detective hat and begin to ask the question "why"? We conduct an archaeological dig and continue to ask why with each layer uncovered until we reach the substrate. Why is there an endless source of poachers? Why is the potential reward greater than the risk? Why is our ethical argument not getting through to them? These aren't rhetorical questions. These are actionable questions meant to lead us deeper into our dive to identify the foundational issue. Once that is uncovered, and only then, can we begin the process of accepting it, understanding it, and transforming it.

Killing Rhinos and Elephants

In endangered species protection, one of the most gut-wrenching challenges of our time is to prevent the unnecessary killing of wildlife as part of the illegal wildlife trade. We have spent millions of dollars and endless hours on preventing poaching, stopping the demand, and educating the public at large about the issue, yet the tragedies continue to arise daily in the news. It is clear we haven't yet dug deep enough into the issue to resolve it. We may have created tunnel vision by labeling the demand as the sole root cause.

It is indeed a key piece to the puzzle. However it is not the only piece. We must be willing to go deeper into the issue to ask the necessary "whys" that will bring us to the additional foundational causes that support the continuation of the problem. This deep dive allows us to redefine the issue as a challenge rather than a problem. In every challenge lies opportunity. Once we ask our "whys" and better understand the base issue, we can reframe the challenge as an opportunity to learn the lesson contained within. By applying the principles of conscious conservation to the issue, we can transform it, resolve it, or dissolve it.

Asking Why

To ask the "whys," begin by identifying a challenge in modern conservation, no matter how big or small. Write it down, define it, and then ask "why." On the next line, answer your question as best you can. Again, follow this with "why?" and answer this as best you can.

Continue answering your "whys" down the page, line by line, until you feel you have landed on the foundational cause. It is here that we wish to focus our efforts. Here is how a deep dive into the poaching crisis might look:

- Rhino poaching crisis. Why?
- Killed illegally for horns. Why?
- Demand in parts of Asia run by syndicates who task locals or insiders to carry out. Why?
- For locals it is lucrative, and there is a need for money, greed,

and lack of respect for wildlife. Why?

- Disobedient of law, may already be engaging in other criminal activity, risk greater than reward, lives in poverty and views poaching as a means to a living, no reverence for life. Why?
- Doesn't value wildlife alive over dead, doesn't respect the law, low likelihood of getting caught or punished, lacks access to skills training and job opportunities, has developed an attitude of apathy. Why?
- Wildlife parts are more lucrative than live wildlife, lack of adequate security measures and poor arrest and prosecution rates, lives in an impoverished community with little to no income streams or revenue, adjacent to an area where wildlife is abundant.

Here we have uncovered three foundational reasons as to why poaching continues. There are more reasons; this is merely an exercise to demonstrate the technique. We can now divide and conquer by focusing on:

- adding value to free-ranging wildlife
- enhancing security measures, enforcement, and prosecution for wildlife crime
- creating job opportunities for communities at the interface.

As you can see, the foundational issues revolve around human problems. Thus it is imperative that we include humans in our conservation efforts and focus more on the human species in crisis as a means to resolving our ecological crises. And we do so by working together as colleagues, rather than in competition with one another for funds and the spotlight. We also play to our own strengths and talents in order to contribute to the challenge. This requires us to tap into our unique skills and abilities and to believe in the power we each possess to make a difference.

Note this is not an exercise in making excuses for those committing the crimes. Rather it is to work toward developing a better understanding of the driving forces behind the action itself. It is simply a tool meant to take us beyond the surface level so that we can address the issue in a sustainable way, at the root, rather than at its many branches.

When we remove our focus from the more superficial aspects of the issue, we open ourselves up to the possibility of thinking creatively about addressing the root cause or causes. When we address the fundamental cause, all other aspects of the challenge dissolve in turn, as they cannot be sustained. Note that root causes are often human-related—psychological, socio-economic, political, cultural, and medical. This is where a multidisciplinary approach benefits us greatly. Humans are a vital component of the global ecology and, by including humans in an ecological framework of conservation, we focus on restoring balance through including humans as part of the solution rather than demanding they merely change their ways. This form of conservation is not traditional in its approach as it focuses on the human species as both the contributor to the issue as well as the solution.

This approach empowers people to change by working with them rather than removing their power and relying on control to force change. We cannot control anyone or anything in the universe. We do however possess the power to influence future outcomes through our own energy, behavior, and contribution to the planet.

Here is an example where a deep dive was applied to a conservation challenge. One of the root causes was identified, and an innovative strategy was implemented in order to transform the situation.

Conservation through public health

Let's take a deep dive into one of modern conservation's success stories, the work of Dr. Gladys Kalema and her charitable organization, Conservation Through Public Health (CTPH). CTPH provides health care services to communities surrounding Virunga National Park, which is home to a portion of the remaining population of endangered mountain gorillas. The region has one of the highest human population densities in Africa. Thus human encroachment is one of the main threats to the gorillas, along with disease transmission from humans and their livestock. Rather than focusing on placing restrictions on community access to the park as a solution to the superficial issue of the need to prevent or limit human contact with gorillas and to restrict the utilization of natural resources in gorilla habitat, Dr. Kalema worked with them to understand their unique troubles and needs. She then adopted a conscious approach to transforming the situation by focusing on humans as part of the ecosystem and part of the solution. She engaged with local communities throughout the search for solutions (transdisciplinarity) and rather than tell them what they couldn't do, she asked the necessary whys and discovered that they lacked access to family planning, which is a root cause for overpopulation and human encroachment that threatens the mountain gorilla population. She also discovered that communities at the interface with mountain gorillas lacked access to adequate health care, including the reduction of infectious disease transmission. This was identified by Dr. Kalema as another root cause for the decline in mountain gorilla populations— the threat of human disease transmission to the gorillas. This exercise in asking "why" was key for both the people as well as the gorillas, as the detrimental effects of habitat loss/encroachment and the pressing human-wildlife disease interface could be mitigated through Dr. Kalema's public health approach to conservation. By addressing the root causes through the provision of women's health care and family planning, infectious disease control, assistance in the development of sustainable income, and education on the importance of gorilla conservation, she is saving gorillas as well as turning communities into advocates for gorilla conservation.[18]

Summary

Takeaways

- Ask why and deep dive into the root cause of issues
- Solving human-based problems is a necessary focus of the modern conscious conservationist
- The lessons of conservation failures will continue to play out until we learn them and transform them
- Use compassion to broaden your understanding of the root issues

Questions for reflection

1. Can you think of a conservation challenge where you have judged or blamed others for the issue rather than accept the situation as it is?
2. Have you asked the necessary "whys" in order to determine the root cause(s)?

Less doing, more being

Often we are busy "doing"—judging others whom we have labeled as bad or wrong and reacting with frustration and anger to the circumstances we dislike. "Doing" is also blaming and shaming others for the current state of affairs and being so busy in our own heads that we miss the lessons in the challenges we face. "Being" requires observing, listening to understand, and sitting in stillness with the issue long enough to know the way forward. It is from this state of being we can take action from a place of clarity and calm in order to collaborate on sustainable solutions that benefit all sides of the conservation equation. Choose a particular challenge you see in conservation and practice a deep dive. Ask the necessary "whys" in order to get to the fundamental or root issue(s). Now address the issue(s) at the base and come up with solutions that will impact the root issue rather than the surface problem.

INTUITIVE CONSERVATION

$\mathcal{W}$hen you reach the end of what you should know, you will be at the beginning of what you should sense.

~Kahlil Gibran

Mind-full vs Mindful

Human beings have extremely cluttered minds, filled with thoughts, memories, worries, and judgments that prevent us from living in the present moment. Our busy schedules and full lives are but a mirror reflection of what is going on in our heads. We are running at full speed and often thinking several steps ahead about what we must do later in the day, the week, the month, or the year, all while missing what is happening right in front of us. We live in a mind-full state—our minds are full with junk.

What is mindfulness? Mindfulness is a purposeful, powerful awareness of the present moment. It is a mentality that creates a feeling of calm by letting go of thoughts that would normally serve to distract us from what is actually happening. It is also an acceptance of the moment as it is, without judgment or the desire to control or change it. It has been referred to as the space between thoughts. It can be fleeting in the beginning, but with practice one can spend more time in the awareness of the present and experience its restorative and healing benefits.

Human beings have highly developed cognitive abilities and have become specialists in thinking. While this has its evolutionary advantages, it most certainly has its misfortunes as well. Along with the ability to analyze comes the tendency to over-analyze. We don't just think, we overthink, obsess, replay, and redirect our emotion and energy to fuel our thoughts, especially negative thoughts. We aren't living up to our full intellectual capacity, the capacity to apply critical thinking to solve the challenges we face. This preoccupation with repetitive and negative thought also distracts us from the complete experience of our spiritual being. Some believe this harkens back to a survival mentality, that we are wired to avoid danger, and thus we have keen awareness and ability to recognize the negative.[19] Unfortunately, our bodies cannot distinguish between real and perceived threats. Thus the negative influences in our lives, whether of critical importance or not, have an additive impact on our physiological stress response. In other words, our negative self-talk is equally as damaging as negative experiences.

Mindfulness is a skill that cannot so much be taught as it must be experienced. With practice it becomes second nature and the individual progresses from "doing" or practicing mindfulness, to "being" or becoming mindful or aware. Mindfulness is a state of being that is available to everyone and can be practiced anywhere and in any situation.

To cultivate mindfulness you can first begin with the realization that you are not your thoughts. You are the observer of the chatter. The goal is not to live in quiet stillness where there is no chatter. Rather it is to become detached from the chatter and to prevent the chatter from ruling your life and your emotions. Over time the chatter will decrease, as you no longer believe that you are your thoughts. Rather you come to know the quiet stillness as the true essence of who you are, your inner self, and that self recognizes the mind as a part of you but not all of you. Your identification with your mind and thus your ego lessens, and you use your intellect as a tool while drawing from your inner strength or inner knowingness as a complement to the intellect.

Benefits of Mindfulness

Mindfulness is known to facilitate general mental well-being and the development of calmness, clarity, and concentration.[20]

The benefits of mindfulness include cognitive gains such as:

- Reduced rumination of thoughts, especially negative thought patterns[21]
- Stress reduction; significantly less anxiety, depression, and somatic distress, i.e. less stress-related cortisol; post-traumatic stress disorder (PTSD) symptoms decreased with meditation[22,23]
- Boosts to working memory[24]
- Improved focus[25]
- Less emotional reactivity[26]
- More cognitive flexibility; meditation also activates the brain region associated with more adaptive responses to stressful or negative situations.[27,28] Activation of this region corresponds

with faster recovery to baseline after being negatively provoked.[29]

- Improved relationships[30]
- Additional benefits include enhanced self-insight, morality, intuition, fear modulation, increased immune functioning,[31] improvement to well-being[32] and reduction in psychological distress.[33] In addition, mindfulness meditation practice appears to increase information-processing speed,[34] as well as decrease task effort and the presence of thoughts that are unrelated to the task at hand.[35]

Psychologically, mindfulness promotes

- Empathy[36]
- Compassion (through non-judgment and non- reactivity)[37]
- Increased patience and gratitude[38]

Mindfulness Cultivates Intuition

By practicing the art of "present awareness," you identify less with the thought cycle continuously running through your mind and more with your inner self, the body and its sensations, and your immediate surroundings. You become more alive as you connect with the present moment through tuning in to all that is happening, including your feelings and intuition, or the inner voice that often emanates from deep within that cannot be explained rationally. Rather it exists as a knowing.

As conservationists, we rely heavily on the use of logic, reasoning, facts, and science. What you may not have considered or appreciated is the little voice deep inside that pushes and sometimes compels you to do something you simply cannot explain. Or the feeling you know the correct action to take regarding a challenge without being able to identify how you know this to be true. The majority of us have likely trained ourselves away from listening to our gut feelings as they relate to our work, so this may be a foreign concept with respect to your work in conservation.

Intuition is something we all have. It is an innate compass that guides us through life, sensing and reading situations distinct from, and often well in advance of, our logical mind. It is known as listening to our gut, relying on instincts, or going on a hunch. It is an inner knowingness that emerges when we take a moment to disconnect from our thinking mind and tune in to our deeper awareness. It is the opposite of logic and reason but can serve as a complement to it. It can enhance scientific knowledge.[39]

Intuition plus science leads to "conservation in action." It is often the key piece to successful conservation endeavors.

The really valuable factor is intuition. ~Albert Einstein

Intuition in Science and Conservation

Humans can use intuition to make faster, more accurate, and more confident decisions.[40] Intuition can be utilized in a number of ways in science, including:

- The creation of hypotheses for research
- Distinguishing truth from opinion in opposing viewpoints
- Determining whether a concept will be successful in reality

versus only on paper

- The art of medicine, i.e. the unexplainable in life, illness, and death
- The social aspects of science, i.e. unpredictability of human and animal nature, and the universe itself

Intuitive Conservation

Published science may not be as much of an absolute truth as we tend to think it is. A hallmark of scientific research is its reproducibility. Yet according to research published as part of a Cancer Reproducibility Project, an estimated 75–90% of scientific experiments published in high-profile, peer-reviewed journals were irreproducible when attempted by biotechnology researchers in California.[41] As with news and social media, published literature is also often a result of the most interesting, unexpected, eye-catching, or novel results, and may represent a cherry-picking of the complete results.

Unfortunately, even the scientific literature is not immune to the sensationalist trends we see in news and social media. This is not to suggest we shouldn't continue to rely on scientific evidence to guide our decision-making in conservation. What it does serve to illustrate, however, is that we cannot rely solely on scientific evidence to guide us in making decisions that play out in the real world. We can enhance our current work in conservation by combining the science of conservation with the art of conservation. We combine our logical, reasoning mind with our intuition or our inner knowingness.

As conservationists, we can fall into the trap of following the money or creating a niche for ourselves (based on funding or popularity), and we stop listening to our intuition rather than ask what is needed, what is practical, and what is sustainable. We also may be guided by our own desires for acknowledgment, fame, recognition, promotion, success, or another self-proposed agenda, rather than utilizing our intuition and continually asking what is best from a conservation standpoint, for ecological health, for biodiversity, for habitat protection, as well as for the communities at the interface.

Characteristics of the non-intuitive conservationist:

- Relies only on scientific facts to determine action; ignores gut, hunches, and instincts
- Neglects their creative side, focusing only on feeding their knowledge through academia, research, and science
- Is constantly in conversation (whether in their own head or with others) or using distractive devices (TV, phone, internet)
- Bases present situations on past experience only, and predicts the future based on past experience
- Makes assumptions and judgments
- Neglects self-care; workaholic

Characteristics of an intuitive conservationist:

- Balances gut with head; i.e. listen to gut, hunches, and instincts
- Taps into creative side; can be through art, hobbies, or innovative approaches to conventional challenges
- Spends time in silence, can be meditation, "mindless" activity, journaling
- Practices mindfulness, i.e. seeing things as they are in present awareness, not through the filter of past or future

- Makes more observations, fewer judgments (doesn't assume)
- Practices self-care, takes time to de-stress

Summary

Takeaways

- Adopt an intuitive approach to conservation
- Balance science with intuition to solve conservation challenges

Questions for reflection

1. Do you rely heavily on logic, reason, science, and facts to guide your work and decision-making in conservation?
2. Can you begin to listen more to your intuition as a complement to your knowledge?

Less doing, more being

"Doing" is often tied to the restless mind, where our rambling thoughts take us to reactive places. You don't "do" mindfulness; you become mindful. It is a state of awareness whereby you tune in to the energy of the present and the energy of the universe, and you tap into your inner knowingness. This shift transcends our tendency to recycle thoughts and to project worry into future events or to dwell on past events. Becoming mindful is a key aspect of conscious conservation. When we are mindful we are focused, we are connected with truth and compassion and with creativity and inspiration. It is from this place we are able to operate with clarity and transform challenges into opportunities.

Focus less on action that is based on scientific knowledge alone and more on the balance between your mind and your intuition. This combination leads to intuitive conservation, or conservation in action. Before you write that next informative blog post, design a fundraising campaign, determine which research focus to take, draw conclusions from research, interpret scientific reporting, or determine which species to prioritize, take some time to be mindful and tune in to your intuition. What is your gut telling you? Don't take everything at face value. When we become inspired, we are more likely to tap into our intuition for guidance, along with our own unique skills, abilities, and creativity to make a positive impact.

THE WAY FORWARD

*N*ature is not a place to visit. It is home.
~Gary Snyder

The Awareness of Animals

Truly, we humans make life so much more difficult, painful, regrettable, undesirable, and insufferable than need be. We could learn valuable lessons on how to become a conscious conservationist by observing the very wildlife that we protect.

Wild animals are the masters of meditation:

- They spend the majority of their lives in quiet peace
- They don't waste time recycling negative thought or dwelling on things
- They experience stress when necessary and quickly return back to a state of homeostasis

- They don't experience depression over the past nor anxiety about the future
- They don't hold grudges or judgments
- They live in a state of awareness, in the present moment

Many humans have very special bonds with animals, bonds that cannot be explained through mere words. This is a soul-to-soul recognition. It exists beyond cognition and without the need to be put into words.

Perhaps our fondness for animals lies in their lack of judgment for us, or because they allow us to give and receive love without condition. They accept us exactly as we are and never demand that we become any more or less. They live in present awareness and do not naturally suffer from anxiety or depression by dwelling in the realm of the past or future (captive animals and domestic animals can suffer these conditions, but it is due to some abnormality of circumstance such as a human-induced trauma or a captive environment). They embody the qualities of non-judgment and acceptance. They do not have an ego. Sounds like precisely the qualities needed for a transformation of consciousness, and just the sort of attributes we need to see in this world. These are the qualities of conscious conservation. It seems that the animals have had it right all along. We could learn a thing or two from them.

In truth, animals utilize more of their sensory abilities than we could ever hope to because they rely less heavily on their cognition and more on the balance between emotion, sensation, thought, and instinct. For example, there are dogs who can detect seizures before they occur or can predict a panic attack in humans with PTSD. Dogs and other animals can access parts of themselves that humans often block because we are so engrossed in our minds.

Animals don't develop an ego identity. Animals don't distinguish between right and wrong. Animals don't judge themselves or others. Animals don't overthink. Yes, there is fighting, competition, life and death, and pain in the world of nature, and yet, it simply is. It exists without the labeling that creates suffering. Pain is a natural sensation, and unavoidable at times; it turns to suffering when we intellectualize it, ruminate on it, recall it, and agonize over it. Suffering relates to the memory of pain and can impact one's life long after the actual sensation of pain has subsided. This is a human quality. Sadly, we now see suffering in some wildlife impacted by human stressors; orphaned wildlife that witness the death of their mothers do indeed experience suffering and psychological trauma that parallels what we know as PTSD in humans. Animals in captivity suffer as a result of being removed from their natural environment, living in suboptimal conditions. But these circumstances are distinctly different from natural pain experienced in the wild, whether from childbirth, illness, injury, or death.

With this in mind, it is clear that we stand to learn a tremendous amount simply by observing and honoring the awareness animals possess. It seems they are quite aware that the present moment is all that they have. It is true some species have the cognitive ability to reflect on past memories. Take elephants, for example, who pay their respects to deceased family members by visiting the "graveyards" where they lie months or even years after their death (here I am referring specifically to elephants who have died of natural causes rather than at the hands of humans). This does not however cause them suffering. Sadness, indeed. But suffering is the result of ruminating on the pain. Elephants don't dwell in this sadness. They honor the life of their family member and thus honor their own emotions and love for family, and for life. The emotion is felt completely and fully, expressed, and in due time they move on.

If you want to know the secret to unlocking your awareness, to raising your consciousness, to living in the present moment, and to becoming a conscious conservationist, it couldn't be simpler. Go to nature. Return to that from which you came. Return to the wild, to the very place from which your inner conservationist was born. Return to the "knowing" you feel when in the presence of the wild. To the awareness that comes from gazing into the eyes of a wild being. Remember the feeling of timelessness. Remember the indescribable, the lack of need for words. The sense of wonderment for creation and for life. It is to that place you must go again if you desire change for the better. It is to the wilderness you must return.

Nature has an abundance of knowledge, but we must be willing to return to our inner awareness in order to hear what she has to say. We must disconnect from our own repetitive thinking in order to connect with the knowing.

We have an abundance of data, facts, thoughts, and theories related to how we must go about saving species and preserving wild spaces. Yet our world continues to dive deeper into crisis. Perhaps it is time to readjust our approach. Each of us holds a knowing that will lead us collectively to a place of healing. We must be courageous enough to look within and patient enough to stay present until the true knowing is revealed. We must allow nature to teach us how to connect with our inner self. With our inner stillness. To the knowingness that is always present.

In every life challenge there exists a lesson. In order to learn the lesson, we must shift our point of view, our mindset, and our approach. We must accept certain inequities in this world. We must accept that poverty exists. We must accept that people will commit crimes and that injustices will happen. We must accept that humans and wildlife will continue to live in conflict with one another.

We must awaken to the present time and see things as they are rather than as we wish them to be. Once we become present to life as it is, there can be acceptance. Acceptance is not a state of being in agreement with current circumstances. Rather, it is a state of no resistance to what is. Acceptance is surrender to what is. This means letting go of our perception of the world, letting go of how we wish things could be, and letting go of the notion that we can control anything in life other than our own state of being. We release the resistance and thus are allowed the freedom to work within the paradigm of reality. It is here that transformation occurs.

With awareness, acceptance, and surrender, we enter a state of clarity and can view things without attachments or labels. It is here the mind opens to the willingness of possibility. In this state of being, hope is born. Fear of the past and present are gone and the creative spirit can thrive. Ideas are born out of a creative mind, ideas that transcend the parameters of the previously labeled challenge. One now sees the former challenge as an opportunity, as a call to action, as a blessing in disguise, and as a lesson to be learned. Where there was once an obstacle, a focus of blame, a reason for suffering, there is now a stepping stone, a focus on understanding, and a reason for compassion.

We no longer have the luxury of prioritizing our own egos and agendas. We no longer have the luxury of blaming and shaming the villains of conservation in order to make ourselves the right and righteous heroes. We no longer have the luxury of only raising awareness or relying on educating the "ignorant" in order to effect change. We no longer have the luxury of relying solely on logic, data, statistics, reason, and argument in order to overcome the global crisis.

We no longer have the luxury of unconscious conservation. The time is now for awakening. The time is now for learning the lesson. If we do not learn, history will repeat itself until the lesson is learned.

If we are always reacting, we cannot be proactive. We allow ourselves to be triggered into reaction and we are pulled away from having the clarity and composure of the present, to bring forth sustainable solutions that are proactive and preventive in their approach.

Men are not prisoners of fate, but only prisoners of their own minds.
~Franklin D Roosevelt

The Prison of the Past

We are at a pivotal moment in conservation whereby we can no longer deny the failures we are witness to. We can no longer suppress the anger, frustration, and the heartbreak we collectively feel as a result of the global ecological destruction we are facing. It is time to recognize that what's in the way *is* the way. The failures, the painful points are precisely where we must dig deeper in order to allow ourselves to feel our grief deeply and sincerely. To mourn what is no longer and to release the pain in order to make way for the possibility of blessings to come. We have to be willing to let go of the failures and the pain of the destruction of the past in order to make room for a new reality and a better tomorrow. We must release the prison of the past in order to learn the lesson it holds for us all. If we do not face these failures with compassion, the lessons will not be learned and thus will continue to play out until we are ready to learn them.

There are both individual and collective lessons to learn. As more individuals learn the lesson, we move closer to the freedom of learning the collective lesson. We gain momentum this way.

We are at the precipice, the turning point. We no longer have the luxury of remaining entrenched in our old ways. We cannot continue to use the same arguments, the same rhetoric, and the same tactics. It is time to break the paradigm and rise. Not only rise to meet the challenges we face, but to rise above them. To surmount them and to raise the bar for conservation as well as our own consciousness. By rising, we will transform ourselves in the process and thus transform the challenges as well. They are ultimately our greatest blessings for they are what will force us to awaken. This awakening may come only after we have seen more destruction and witnessed more tragedy, more death, and more loss. Or this awakening can happen in the present time, preventing future destruction, tragedy, and loss. It can eternally disrupt the endless cycle of the zero-sum game.

The power lies within each of us to determine the outcome.

Return to Compassion

We must become familiar with the root causes of the challenges of modern conservation by being present and aware, removing the labels of right/wrong and good/evil, and letting go of the zero-sum mentality. When we become aware, we become clear and think critically about the circumstances without judgment. We develop a willingness to dive deeper. We waste less time working to fix the superficial issues and instead focus on the root issue. Often the root cause is human derived. Thus we must place our focus on understanding the driving emotions behind the issue, from the human perspective. This is where compassion comes in. We cannot always fix our way through the challenge. We must become compassionate enough to understand and to support those impacted directly by the challenge so that they are empowered to transform the challenge into an opportunity. We must become still long enough to truly listen to the other side so we can understand, rather than just to retort.

The lessons are simple yet have become chronically distorted, magnified, and compounded over time. The greatest lesson we can learn that will help rebalance our planet, save species, and slow the tide of anthropogenic destruction is to return to compassion. Changing the world we live in begins by changing ourselves, as our inner self is ultimately the only thing we have the power to change. We mustn't underestimate the power that lies within each of us to transform, and thus to transform our world as a result.

There is nothing in this world that cannot be healed through the power of compassion.

Be the Change

Make a commitment to be the resolution. To observe what is missing in the world as an invitation to become that which is required.

At its essence, conservation is simply a deep reverence for life in all its various forms. Conservation is not merely preservation for the sake of preserving. Rather it is about honoring the space we share as beings in the world and allowing the balance to be achieved by a powerful reverence for Mother Nature.

It is an honoring of the life force within each of us and a recognition that humans are inextricably tied to the life force of nature. We cannot live without wilderness.

What is currently playing out on the global environmental stage is merely a reflection of what is going on inside us. We have become enslaved to our egos and have abandoned the beautiful parts of our essence in exchange for the superficialities of this world, and in return we see the destruction of the world around us.

We must relearn to surrender, both within and without. We must surrender within to our true innermost self. It is here where we will find the clarity, inspiration, and compassion necessary to transform the world. We must also surrender to nature in order to learn her lessons. In order to heal our planet, to save species, and to preserve life, we must first heal ourselves. We as a species cannot survive otherwise.

If we are going to see the change, we must be the change. Each of us has within an endless supply of intuition and compassion that can be utilized to solve the challenges we face in conservation. Your intuition and compassion can be accessed through mindfulness, through the power of the present moment. We are losing precious time by dwelling on the past and fretting over the future. Conscious conservation is grounded in the present.

Conscious conservation is a path to becoming the embodiment of that which you wish to see in the world. In order for it to happen, you must be present, intuitive, compassionate, and ever-hopeful in the return to a balanced earth. You must believe in the power of the human species to transform into the guardians of the planet, reintegrated into nature as we were meant to be. You must believe in Mother Nature's power to heal, if we can only give her the chance. You must believe in humanity once again. Finally, you must believe in yourself, as it is deep within where you will find the power to create a world we can all be proud of.

NOTES

 hapter 1

1. Kolbert, *The Sixth Extinction: An Unnatural History*, 3.

Chapter 2

2. "Jane Goodall." Wikipedia. https://en.wikipedia.org/wiki/Jane_GoodallChapter

3. "Lion Lights." Wikipedia. https://en.wikipedia.org/wiki/Lion_lights

Chapter 4

4. Cacioppo, "May I Have Your Attention, Please: Electrocortical Responses to Positive and Negative Stimuli," 171.

5. King, "Beehive Fences As a Multidimensional Conflict-Mitigation Tool for Farmers Coexisting with Elephants," 752.

6. Huzzah, "Efficacy of Two Lion Conservation Programs in Maasailand, Kenya," 851.

7. Lewis, "Community Markets for Conservation (COMACO) Links Biodiversity Conservation with Sustainable Improvements in Livelihoods and Food Production," 13958.

Chapter 6

8. Kristeller, "Science Looks at Spirituality - Cultivating Loving Kindness: A Two-Stage Model of the Effects of Meditation on Empathy, Compassion, and Altruism," 399-400.

Chapter 9

9. Silvia, "Deflecting Reactance: The Role of Similarity in Increasing Compliance and Reducing Resistance," 277. Berger, "What Makes Online Content Viral?," 201.

Chapter 10

10. Berger, "What Makes Online Content Viral?," 201.

11. Seu, "Public Knowledge, Reactions and Moral Actions and Response to Humanitarian Issues," 5-6.

12. Baumeister, "How Emotion Shapes Behavior: Feedback, Anticipation, and Reflection, Rather than Direct Causation," 193-194.

13. Gielan, "Broadcasting Happiness: The Science of Igniting and Sustaining Positive Change, 251-252.

14. Vaish, "Not All Emotions Are Created Equal: The Negativity Bias in Social-Emotional Development," 384.

15. Hooper, "Compassion Satisfaction, Burnout, and Compassion Fatigue Among Emergency Nurses Compared With Nurses in Other Selected Inpatient Specialties," 421.

16. Ochoa-Ochoa, "Distanciation: A Key Challenge for 21st Century Conservation," 207.

17. "Wildlife Crime Tech Challenge," https://wildlifecrimetech.org/index, (retrieved August 22, 2017).

Chapter 11

18. Kalema-Zikusoka, "Sharing the Forest, Protecting Gorillas and Helping Families in Uganda," 4-5.

Chapter 12

19. Vaish, "Not All Emotions Are Created Equal: The Negativity Bias in Social-Emotional Development," 384.

20. Walsh, "The Meeting of Meditative Disciplines and Western Psychology," 229.

21. Chambers, "The Impact of Intensive Mindfulness Training on Attentional Control, Cognitive Style, and Affect," 305.

22. Hofmann, "The Effect of Mindfulness-Based Therapy on Anxiety and Depression: A Meta-Analytic Review," 170.

23. Boden, "Changes in Facets of Mindfulness and Posttraumatic Stress Disorder Treatment Outcome," 612.

24. Jha, "Examining the Protective Effects of Mindfulness Training on Working Memory Capacity and Affective Experience," 62.

25. Moore, "Meditation, Mindfulness and Cognitive Flexibility," 177.

26. Ortner, "Mindfulness Meditation and Reduced Emotional Interference on a Cognitive Task," 271.

27. Cahn, "Meditation States and Traits: EEG, ERP, and Neuroimaging Studies," 181.

28. Davidson, "Alterations in Brain and Immune Function Produced by Mindfulness Meditation," 569.

29. Davidson, "Emotion, Plasticity, Context, and Regulation: Perspectives from Affective Neuroscience," 896.

30. Barnes, "The Role of Mindfulness in Romantic Relationship Satisfaction and Responses to Relationship Stress," 482.

31. Davidson, "Alterations in Brain and Immune Function Produced by Mindfulness Meditation," 569.

32. Carmody, "Relationships between Mindfulness Practice and Levels of Mindfulness, Medical and Psychological Symptoms and Well-Being in a Mindfulness-Based Stress Reduction Program," 31.

33. Bowen, "Mindfulness Meditation and Substance Use in an Incarcerated Population," 352.

34. Moore, "Meditation, Mindfulness and Cognitive Flexibility," 183.

35. Lutz, "Mental Training Enhances Attentional Stability: Neural and Behavioral Evidence," 13426.

36. Birnie, "Exploring Self-compassion and Empathy in the Context of Mindfulness-based Stress Reduction (MBSR)," 359.

37. Shapiro, "Teaching Self-Care to Caregivers: Effects of Mindfulness-Based Stress Reduction on the Mental Health of Therapists in Training," 111.

38. Rothaupt, "Counselors' and Counselor Educators' Practice of Mindfulness: A Qualitative Inquiry," 46,49.

39. Welsh, "Evidence-Based Care and the Case for Intuition and Tacit Knowledge in Clinical Assessment and Decision Making in Mental Health Nursing Practice: An Empirical Contribution to the Debate," 304-305.

40. Lufityanto, "Measuring Intuition: Nonconscious Emotional Information Boosts Decision Accuracy and Confidence," 632.

41. Begley, "Reproducibility in Science: Improving the Standard for Basic and Preclinical Research," 116.

BIBLIOGRAPHY

*A*dams, William. "People, Parks, and Poverty: Political Ecology and Biodiversity Conservation." *Conservation and Society* 5, no. 2 (2007): 147-183.

Baker, Monya. "Cancer Reproducibility Project Releases First Results." *Nature* 541, no. 7637 (2017): 269- 270.

Barnes, Sean. "The Role of Mindfulness in Romantic Relationship Satisfaction and Responses to Relationship Stress." *Journal of Marital and Family Therapy* 33, no. 4 (2007): 482-500.

Baumeister, Roy. "How Emotion Shapes Behavior: Feedback, Anticipation, and Reflection, Rather than Direct Causation." *Personality and Social Psychology Review* 11, no. 2 (2007): 167-203.

Begley, C. Glenn. "Reproducibility in Science: Improving the Standard for Basic and Preclinical Research." *Circulation Research* 116, no. 1 (2015): 116.

Berger, Jonah. "What Makes Online Content Viral?" *Journal of Marketing Research* 49, no. 2 (2012): 192-205.

Birnie, Kathryn. "Exploring Self-Compassion and Empathy in the Context of Mindfulness-Based Stress Reduction (MBSR)." *Stress and Health* 26, no. 5 (2010): 359–371.

Boden, Tyler. "Changes in Facets of Mindfulness and Posttraumatic Stress Disorder Treatment Outcome." *Psychiatry Research* 200, (2012): 609-613.

Bowen, Sarah. "Mindfulness Meditation and Substance Use in an Incarcerated Population." *Psychology of addictive behaviors* 20, no. 3 (2006): 343-347.

Brulle, Robert. "Shifting Public Opinion on Climate Change: An Empirical Assessment of Factors Influencing Concern over Climate Change in the U.S., 2002–2010." *Journal of Climatic Change* 114, no. 2 (2012): 169-188.

Cacioppo, John. "May I Have Your Attention, Please: Electrocortical Responses to Positive and Negative Stimuli." *Neuropsychologia* 41, no. 2 (2003): 171-183.

Cahn, Rael. "Meditation States and Traits: EEG, ERP, and

Neuroimaging Studies." *Psychological bulletin* 132, no. 2 (2006): 180-211.

Carmody, James. "Relationships between Mindfulness Practice and Levels of Mindfulness, Medical and Psychological Symptoms and Well-Being in a Mindfulness-Based Stress Reduction Program." *Journal of Behavioral Medicine* 31, no. 1 (2008): 23-33.

Chambers, Richard. "The Impact of Intensive Mindfulness Training on Attentional Control, Cognitive Style, and Affect." *Cognitive Therapy and Research* 32, no. 3 (2008): 303-322.

Davidson, Richard. "Emotion, Plasticity, Context, and Regulation: Perspectives from Affective Neuroscience." *Psychological bulletin* 126, no. 6 (2000): 890-909.

Davidson, Richard. "Alterations in Brain and Immune Function Produced By Mindfulness Meditation." *Psychosomatic medicine* 65, no. 4 (2003): 564-570.

Davis, Daphne. "What Are the Benefits of Mindfulness? A Practice Review of Psychotherapy-Related Research." *American Psychological Association* 48, no. 2 (2011): 198-208.

Gielan, Michelle. *Broadcasting Happiness: The Science of Igniting and Sustaining Positive Change*. Dallas: BenBella Books, 2015.

Goodall, Jane. *Through a Window: My Thirty Years with the Chimpanzees of Gombe*. Boston: Houghton Mifflin, 1990.

Hofmann, Stefan. "The Effect of Mindfulness- Based Therapy on Anxiety and Depression: A Meta- Analytic Review." *Journal of Consulting and Clinical Psychology* 78, no. 2 (2010): 169-183.

Hooper, Crystal. "Compassion Satisfaction, Burnout, and Compassion Fatigue Among Emergency Nurses Compared with Nurses in Other Selected Inpatient Specialties." *Journal of Emergency Nursing* 36, no. 5 (2010): 420-427.

Huzzah, Leela. "Efficacy of Two Lion Conservation Programs in Maasailand, Kenya." *Conservation Biology* 28, no. 3 (2014): 851-860.

"Jane Goodall." Wikipedia. https://en.wikipedia.org/wiki/Jane_Goodall (retrieved August 22, 2017).

Jha, Amishi. "Examining the Protective Effects of Mindfulness Training on Working Memory Capacity and Affective Experience." American Psychological Association 10, no. 1 (2010): 54-64.

Kalema-Zikusoka, Gladys. "Sharing the Forest, Protecting Gorillas and Helping Families in Uganda." *Focus series, published by the Woodrow Wilson International Centre for International Scholars and USAID.* 17 (2008): 1-7.

King, Lucy. "Beehive Fences as a Multidimensional Conflict-Mitigation Tool for Farmers Coexisting with Elephants." *Conservation biology: the Journal of the Society for Conservation Biology* 31, no. 4 (2017): 743-752.

Kolbert, Elizabeth. *The Sixth Extinction: An Unnatural History*. New York: Henry Holt and Company, 2014.

Kristeller, JL, and T Johnson. "Science Looks at Spirituality—Cultivating Loving Kindness: A Two-Stage Model of the Effects of Meditation on Empathy, Compassion, And Altruism." *Zygon* 40, no. 2 (n.d.): 391-407.

Lewis, Dale. "Community Markets for Conservation (COMACO) Links Biodiversity Conservation with Sustainable Improvements in Livelihoods and Food Production." *PNAS* 108, no. 34 (2011): 13957-13962.

"Lion Lights." Wikipedia. https://en.wikipedia.org/wiki/Lion_lights (retrieved August 22, 2017).

Lufityanto, Galang. "Measuring Intuition: Nonconscious Emotional Information Boosts Decision Accuracy and Confidence." *Psychological Science* 27, no. 5 (2016): 622-634.

Lutz, Antoine. "Mental Training Enhances Attentional Stability: Neural and Behavioral Evidence." *The Journal of Neuroscience: the official journal of the Society for Neuroscience* 29, no. 42 (2009): 13418-13427.

Moeller, Susan. *Compassion Fatigue: How the Media Sell Disease, Famine, War, and Death.* New York: Routledge, 1999.

Moore, Adam. "Meditation, Mindfulness and Cognitive Flexibility." *Consciousness and cognition* 18, no. 1 (2009): 176-186.

Ochoa-Ochoa, Leticia. "Distanciation: A Key Challenge for 21st Century Conservation." *29th International Conference on Informatics for Environmental Protection (EnviroInfo 2015).* 207-212.

O'Malley, Mary. *What's In the Way, Is the Way: Moving beyond Your Struggle into the Joy of Being Alive.* Kirkland: Awaken Publications, 2013.

Ortner, Catherine. "Mindfulness Meditation and Reduced Emotional Interference on a Cognitive Task." *Motivation and Emotion* 31, no. 4 (2007): 271-283.

Rothaupt, Jeanne. "Counselors' and Counselor Educators' Practice of Mindfulness: A Qualitative Inquiry." *Counseling and Values* 52, no. 1 (2007): 40-54.

Schwartz, Jeffrey. *You Are Not Your Brain: The 4- Step Solution for Changing Bad Habits, Ending Unhealthy Eating, and Taking Control of Your Life.* New York: Avery, 2012.

Seu, Bruna. *Public Knowledge, Reactions and Moral Actions in Response to Humanitarian Issues.* Summary Findings of Focus Groups Conducted in the UK in 2011 – Interim Report 2. 1-55.

Shapiro, Shauna. "Teaching Self-Care to Caregivers: Effects of Mindfulness-Based Stress Reduction on the Mental Health of Therapists in Training." *Training and Education in Professional Psychology* 1, no. 2 (2007): 105-115.

Silvia, Paul. "Deflecting Reactance: The Role of Similarity in Increasing Compliance and Reducing Resistance." *Basic and Applied Social Psychology* 27 (2005): 277–284.

Taylor, Jill. *My Stroke of Insight: A Brain Scientist's Personal Journey.* New York: Viking, 2008.

Tolle, Eckhart. *The Power of Now: A Guide to Spiritual Enlightenment.* Vancouver, B.C: Namaste Pub, 2004.

Vaish, Amrisha. "Not All Emotions Are Created Equal: The Negativity Bias in Social-Emotional Development." *Psychological Bulletin* 134, no. 3 (2008): 383-403.

van der Linden, Sander. "Improving Public Engagement with Climate Change: Five "Best Practice" Insights from Psychological Science." *Perspectives on Psychological Science* 10, no. 6 (2015): 758-763.

Waelde, Lynn. "A Pilot Study of Meditation for Health Care Workers

Following Hurricane Katrina." *Journal of Traumatic Stress* 21, no. 5 (2008): 497-500.

Walsh, Roger. "The Meeting of Meditative Disciplines and Western Psychology." *American Psychologist* 61, no. 3 (2006): 227-239.

Welsh, I. "Evidence-Based Care and the Case for Intuition and Tacit Knowledge in Clinical Assessment and Decision Making in Mental Health Nursing Practice: An Empirical Contribution to the Debate." *Journal of Psychiatric and Mental Health Nursing* 8, no. 4 (2001): 299-305.

"Wildlife Crime Tech Challenge," https://wildlifecrimetech.org/index (retrieved August 22, 2017)

www.drhayleyadams.com

@drhayleyadams

hayley@drhayleyadams.com

ABOUT THE AUTHOR

Dr. Adams has over 20 years of experience in wildlife veterinary medicine, conservation, and issues related to One Health in Africa, and has thoroughly enjoyed working with a variety of domestic and wild animals over the years. She has a particular interest in empowering others to believe they alone can make this world a better place for all beings. She created a charitable organization, Silent Heroes Foundation, in 2010 as a way of contributing to conservation & One Health efforts in Africa. She is a veterinarian and holds PhD in wildlife epidemiology and virology. She is also a board certified Diplomate in the American College of Veterinary Preventive Medicine and the American College of Veterinary Microbiology. She currently teaches conservation medicine and related courses at the University of Florida.

For more information please visit

drhayleyadams.com
hayley@drhayleyadams.com

Made in the USA
Columbia, SC
10 August 2021